Grammar Matters
RIDDLES

The Sterling Book of Riddles is a scintillating amalgamation of riddles of all shades and hues — old and new, simple and complex, gags and brain-teasers, puns and conundrums. This amazing range of riddles in this collection will not only provide you with endless hours of amusement but also stimulate intellectual growth.

Gratian Vas has a master's degree in English Literature from Delhi University. With a vast experience in the field of education, he has a number of books in General English to his credit.

BOOKS IN ENGLISH LANGUAGE LEARNING SERIES

Grammer Matters

Common Errors in English

Dictionary for Misspellers

Idioms

Quotations

Proverbs

Riddles

Tongue Twisters

The Complete Guide to

Business Letters

Effective English Writing

Essays for Competitive
  Examinations

Functional Writing in English

Modern Essays

Paragraph to Essay Writing

Prose Compositions

Résumé Writing

Letters for Social Interaction

Enrich your Grammar

Antonyms

Current Words and Phrases

Prepositions

Synonyms

Word Perfect

Word Power

Word to Paragraph

Words and Their Usages

Word Origins

Communications Skills

The Power of Spoken English
  (with 2 audio CDs)

Speaking and Writing in English

Dynamic Reading Skills

Effective Communication

English Conversation Practice

How to Develop Profitable
  Listening Skills

How to Increase Your Reading
  Speed

How to Listen Better

How to Read Effectively and
  Efficiently

How to Resolve Conflicts

Grammar Matters
RIDDLES

GRATIAN VAS

STERLING PAPERBACKS
An imprint of
Sterling Publishers (P) Ltd.
A-59, Okhla Industrial Area, Phase-II,
New Delhi-110020.
Tel: 26387070, 26386209; Fax: 91-11-26383788
E-mail: sterlingpublishers@airtelmail.in
ghai@nde.vsnl.net.in
www.sterlingpublishers.com

Grammar Matters: Riddles
© 2006, Sterling Publishers Pvt. Ltd.
ISBN 978-81-207-1865-4
Reprint 2007, 2009, 2010, 2011, 2012

Printed and Published by Sterling Publishers Pvt. Ltd.,
New Delhi-110 020.

PREFACE

A riddle is a puzzling question or a proposition put in obscure or ambiguous terms to puzzle you or make you exercise your ingenuity in discovering its meaning.

Riddles are based on language and logic. They are not bound by any complicated rules. To ask a riddle, all you need to do is to communicate with someone capable of understanding what you say.

The English language has a large number of words with more than one meaning and also words with similar pronunciation. These words provide the material for most riddles.

What tongue never speaks?
The tongue in your shoe.

What vegetable is dangerous if found on board a ship?
A leek (leak).

Riddles present an excellent and immensely popular form of verbal play. They teach us something we did not know before about words or about logical relationships, making them an entertaining learning experience.

The fun is in asking a riddle. Amusement comes from the fact that the straight or obvious answer always turns out to be the wrong one!

What is a dimple?
A pimple going the other way.

Gratian Vas

Riddles 1-250

1. A barrel of beer fell on a brewery worker. Why wasn't he hurt?

2. A butcher is 6 feet tall and wears size 9 shoes. What does he weigh?

3. A trapper sheltering in a shack in the freezing cold found a fireplace with well-laid wood and twigs, a full oil-lamp, a candle and a matchbox with a single matchstick. Which must he light first to save himself from freezing?

4. A postman, a fireman, a chef and a policeman wear hats. Which one wears the largest?

5. A man was about to hit somebody. Why was he like a clock with hands at 12.59?

6. A girl kissed and hugged a man at the station. When questioned, she said 'Why not? He is the only son of my mother's mother-in-law.' Who was he?

7. A farmer had 20 sheep. All but 9 died. How many did he have left?

8. A knight in armour had a pain. When and where was it?

9. A little thing, a pretty thing, without a top or bottom. What am I?

10. A farmer had eggs for breakfast every morning. He owned no chickens and didn't get eggs from anybody else. Where did he get the eggs?

11. A forest is two kilometres across. How far can you go into it?

12. A man had two sons and named them both Ed? Why?

13. A lady who works in a sweet shop in Cambridge has measurements of 40-26-40. She is 5 feet 4 inches tall and wears a size 9 shoe. What do you think she weighs?

14. A man was driving a black lorry. His lights were not on, the moon was not out. A lady was crossing the street. How did the driver see her?

15. A man drove from London to Dover with a flat tyre. Why didn't he find this out?

16. A word contains five syllables. Take one away—not one remains.

17. A cabbage, a tap and a tomato had a race. How did it go?

18. A policeman saw a lorry driver going the wrong way down a one-way street, but didn't stop him. Why not?

19. A man and a dog were going down the street. The man rode, yet walked. What was the dog's name?

20. A man who worked in the butcher shop was 6 feet tall, had red hair and wore size 11 shoes. What did he weigh?

21. An elephant always remembers, but what kind of animal always forgets?

22. As long as I eat, I live; but when I drink, I die. What am I?

23. At this moment everyone in the world is doing the same thing. What is it?

24. At what sports do waiters excel?

25. Aunt Mabel has four daughters. Each daughter has a brother, but no father. How many are there in the family—including Uncle Bill and wife?

26. Betty's dog goes for a walk with her. It does not walk in front of her, behind her, or at one side of her. Where does it walk?

27. Born at the same time as the world, will live as long as the world, yet never five weeks old? What is it?

28. Can you make a fire with only one stick?

29. Captain Cook made three voyages round the world and was killed on one of them. Which one?

30. Can a shoe box?

31. Can February march?

32. Can you spell Brandy with three letters?

33. Can you spell soft and slow with two letters?

34. Can you spell very happy with three letters?

35. Can you spell a composition with two letters?
36. Can you spell a pretty girl with two letters?
37. Can you read the following?

    Yy u r yy u b
    I c u r yy 4 me.

38. Did you hear the story about the influenza germ?
39. Did the rooster fall in love with the hen at first sight?
40. Did you hear about the little boy called Nicholas?
41. Did you hear about the Irish dog which sat down to gnaw a bone?
42. Did you hear about the car with the wooden engine and the wooden wheels?
43. Did you hear the joke about the field of corn that was 100 feet high?
44. Did you hear about the Irish caterpillar?
45. Did you hear about the red sauce chasing the brown sauce?
46. Did Cain hate his brother forever?
47. Did you hear the joke about the roof?
48. Did you hear about the stupid water-polo player?
49. Did you hear about the stupid tap-dancer?
50. Did you hear the story about the two holes in the ground?
51. Did you hear the story about the peacock?
52. Did you hear the story about the dust-cart?
53. Did you hear the story about the skunk?
54. Did you hear the story about the burp?
55. Did Adam and Eve ever have a date?
56. Do you say, "Nine and five is thirteen", or "Nine and five are thirteen?"
57. Do moths cry?
58. Dogs have fleas. What do sheep have?
59. Do you know the story of the red-hot poker?
60. Do you believe in clubs for young people?
61. Do sailors go on safaris?
62. Do robots have brothers?

63. Do you know the joke about the rope?
64. Do you know the joke about the umbrella?
65. Do you know the joke about the dirty window?
66. Why are good intentions like fainting ladies?
67. Do you know what Zulus do with banana skins?
68. Do Americans pronounce the second day of the week as Toozday or Chewsday?
69. Do you know the joke about the bed?
70. Do you know how to make a bandstand?
71. Do you know how long cows should be milked?
72. During what season do ants eat most?
73. From what word of eight letters can you extract five and leave ten?
74. From what number can you take half and leave nothing?
75. From a word of five letters take two and leave one.
76. Have you heard the story about the slippery eel?
77. Have you heard the joke about the wall?
78. Have you ever seen a salad bowl?
79. Have you heard the story about the peacock?
80. Have you heard the joke about the butter?
81. Have you heard the story of the church bell?
82. Have you heard the joke about the dog that walked twice from Land's End to John O'Groats?
83. Have you heard the story about the Manx cat?
84. How was it that a dog tied to a 2-foot rope, managed to walk 30 feet?
85. How could you fall off a ten-metre ladder and not be hurt?
86. How can you make a slow horse fast?
87. How would you avoid starvation on a desert island?
88. How did Little Bo-peep lose her sheep?
89. How can a leopard change his spots?
90. How do you know when night is nigh?
91. How do you take a sick pig to hospital?
92. How would you define a stick of rhubarb?

93. How do you make gold soup?
94. How do pixies eat?
95. How do you cut through the waves?
96. How can you put on weight easily?
97. How did the glow-worm feel when it backed into a fan?
98. What's the definition of debate?
99. How can you avoid falling hair?
100. How do you get rid of varnish?
101. How do you make a cigarette lighter?
102. How do barbers get to their shops quickly?
103. How many coats can you get in an empty wardrobe?
104. How does a ship listen?
105. How do you get two whales in a Mini?
106. How do you keep an idiot waiting?
107. How do you make a coat last?
108. How do you know when you're in bed with an elephant?
109. How do you start a teddy-bear race?
110. How did the exhausted sparrow land safely?
111. Where would you find a prehistoric cow?
112. How does an octopus go into battle?
113. How did Noah see the animals in the Ark?
114. How can you communicate with a fish?
115. How do you stop a cockerel crowing on Sunday?
116. How do you start a flea race?
117. How many sides has a circle?
118. How do you stop a dog from barking in the back seat of a car?
119. How do you milk a mouse?
120. How do frogs and rabbits make beer?
121. How do you make a thin guinea-pig fat?
122. How many balls of string would it take to reach the Moon?
123. How would you describe beans on toast?
124. How can you get a quart of milk into a pint-pot?
125. How do fireflies start a race?

126. How can you knock over a full glass without spilling any water?

127. How many days of the week start with the letter T?

128. How does a professional hypnotist travel?

129. How can you always tell an undertaker?

130. How can you tell one sort of cat from another?

131. How do you make notes of stone?

132. How can you go without sleep for seven days and not be tired?

133. How many peas are there in a pod?

134. How did the inventor discover gunpowder?

135. How many acorns grow on the average pine tree?

136. How many weeks belong to the year?

137. How do you spell blind pig?

138. How can you tell the naked truth?

139. How many months have 28 days?

140. How can you leave a room with two legs and return with six legs?

141. How many letters are there in the alphabet?

142. How did the boy feel after being caned?

143. How can you make money fast?

144. How many legs does a mule have if you call its tail a leg?

145. How many wives can an Englishman have?

146. How do we know that S is a scary letter?

147. How long will an eight-day clock run without winding?

148. How many times can 16 be subtracted from 160?

149. How can you keep from getting a sharp pain in your eye when you drink your tea?

150. How can you place a pencil on the floor so that no one can jump over it?

151. How can you come face-to-face with a hungry, angry lion, dare him to fight, and still be unafraid?

152. How do sailors get their clothes clean?

153. How do you keep food on an empty stomach?

154. How do they dance in Saudi Arabia?
155. How can you always find a liar out?
156. How do you make a Maltes Cross?
157. How was the blind carpenter able to see?
158. How do you make an egg roll?
159. How can you double your money?
160. How do you know that carrots are for the eyes?
161. How do you get down from an elephant?
162. How does the letter A help a deaf woman?
163. How did the chicken farmer get up in the morning?
164. How is a pig like a horse?
165. How can you tell a sausage doesn't like being friends?
166. How can you tell twin witches apart?
167. How did the man feel when he got a big bill from the electric company?
168. How can you tell the difference between a can of chicken soup and a can of tomato soup?
169. How do you file a nail?
170. How do you make a lemon drop?
171. How does a baby ghost cry?
172. How can you name the capital of every U.S. state in two seconds?
173. How does a broom act?
174. How can you make seven even?
175. How do mountains hear?
176. How much is 5Q and 5Q?
177. How can you spell rot with two letters?
178. How do you spell "we" with two letters without using the letters W and E?
179. How many ghosts are there in the nation?
180. How can you tell if a mummy has a cold?
181. How did the clock feel when no one wound it up?
182. How did the bread feel when it was put in the toaster?
183. How did the kid get a flat nose?

184. How did the skeleton know it was raining?
185. How can you tell if you are cross-eyed?
186. How do you know that army sergeants have a lot of headaches?
187. How can you tell if a bucket is not well?
188. How are a bad boy and a canoe alike?
189. How do you make Mexican chilli?
190. How can you tell if there is an elephant sleeping in your bed?
191. How can you keep a barking dog quiet?
192. How do you know if soda is any good?
193. How is a bell obedient?
194. How can you tell if there is an elephant in the refrigerator?
195. How can you tell if an elephant has been in the refrigerator?
196. How does a hot dog speak?
197. How did the girl zombie know the boy zombie liked her?
198. How can you get rich by eating?
199. How can you calm down an angry dragon breathing smoke and fire?
200. How can you shorten a bed?
201. How can you eat an egg without your breaking its shell?
202. How can you tell where a bear lives?
203. How do birds stop themselves in the air?
204. How did the big mountain know that the little mountain was fibbing?
205. How do you know that bees are happy?
206. How can you tune into the sun?
207. How can you tell that a cat likes the rain?
208. How do rabbits keep their fur neat?
209. How can you fix a short circuit?
210. How can you spell too much with two letters?
211. How did the 800-pound man feel when he lost 250 pounds?

212. How does a witch tell the time?
213. How does a coffee pot feel when it is hot?
214. How can you make my watch a stopwatch?
215. How can you make a soup rich?
216. How does a pair of pants feel when it is ironed?
217. How do you make a Venetian blind?
218. How can you tell when there is an elephant in your sandwich?
219. How do you fit five elephants into a Volkswagon?
220. How many skunks does it take to make a big stink?
221. How can you drop an egg 3 feet without breaking it?
222. How can you be sure you have counterfeit money?
223. How should you treat a baby goat?
224. How do we know Rome was built at night?
225. How much dirt is there in a hole exactly one foot deep and one foot across?
226. How is a burning candle like thirst?
227. How are 2 plus 2 equal 5 and your left hand alike?
228. How many worms make a foot?
229. How many feet are in a yard?
230. How do we know that mountain goats have feet?
231. I move, but have no legs. I write, but I am not a pen or pencil. I make a noise like a clock, but I am not one. Who am I?
232. I went to a field and couldn't get through it, so I went to a school and learned how to do it. What am I?
233. I can be heard and caught but never seen. What am I?
234. If a man born an Australian, worked in America and died in Europe, what is he?
235. If all of Ireland should sink, what city would remain afloat?
236. If you want to learn to fight, what book should you read?
237. If a flea and a fly pass each other, what time is it?
238. If 3 cats can kill 3 rats in 3 minutes, how long will it take 100 cats to kill 100 rats?

239. If your clock strikes thirteen, what time is it?

240. 'If a fellow met a fibber in a fallow field' - how many 'f's in that?

241. If a red house is made of red bricks and a yellow house is made of yellow bricks, what is a green house made of?

242. If sixteen boys share a chocolate cake, what is the time?

243. If a man has ten sons and each son has a sister, how many children has he altogether?

244. If two is company and three is a crowd, what's four and five?

245. If a man takes one minute to cut through a plank of wood, how long will he take to cut a 10-ft plank into 10 pieces?

246. If a clock takes 2 seconds to strike 2 o'clock, how long does it take to strike 3 o'clock?

247. If the only sister of your mother's only brother, had only child, what is that child to you?

248. If a buttercup is yellow, what colour is a hiccup?

249. If we get honey from a bee, what do we get from wasp?

250. If a runner gets athlete's foot, what does a Roman Catholic Priest get?

Answers

1. 'Cos it was full of light ale.

2. Meat, of course.

3. The match, of course.

4. The one who has the biggest head.

5. They were both on the point of striking one.

6. Her father.

7. 9.

8. In the middle of the (k) night.

9. A diamond ring.

10. From his ducks.

11. One kilometre. After that, you will be going out.

12. He thought two heads were better than one.

13. She weighs sweets.

14. It was a bright, sunny day.

15. It was his spare tyre.

16. Monosyllable. Take away MO and leave NO SYLLABLE.

17. The cabbage was ahead, the tap was running, and the tomato tried to ketchup.

18. The lorry-driver was walking.
19. Yet.
20. Meat.
21. An owl because it keeps saying, "Who? Who?"
22. Fire.
23. Getting older.
24. Tennis. They really know how to serve.
25. 8.
26. On the other side of her.
27. The moon.
28. Yes, providing it's a matchstick.
29. The last one.
30. No, but a tin can.
31. No, April May.
32. B, R, and Y.
33. EZ.
34. XTC (ecstasy).
35. SA (essay)
36. QT (cutey).
37. Too wise you are, too wise you be,

    I see you are too wise for me.
38. Never mind. I don't want to spread it.
39. Not really—she egged him on a bit.
40. He was called Nicholas because he never wore any knickers.
41. When it got up it only had three legs....
42. It wooden go.
43. You wouldn't like it—it's a very tall story.
44. It turned into a frog.
45. It couldn't ketchup.
46. No, just for as long as he was Abel.
47. It's way above your head.
48. His horse drowned....
49. He fell in the sink.
50. Well, well.
51. It's a beautiful tail.
52. It was a load of rubbish.
53. Never mind, it stinks.
54. Never mind. It's not worth repeating.
55. No, they had an apple.
56. Neither. Nine and five are fourteen.
57. Sure. Haven't you ever seen a mothball (bawl)?
58. Fleece.
59. You couldn't grasp it.
60. Only when kindness fails.
61. Not safaris I know.
62. No, only transistors.
63. Aw, skip it....
64. It'd be over your head.
65. You wouldn't see through it.
66. They need carrying out.
67. Throw them away, of course....
68. Almost certainly as Monday.
69. It hasn't been made yet.
70. Take away their chairs.
71. In the same way as short ones.
72. Summer. That is when they go to a lot of picnics.

73. Tendency.

74. The number 8. Take away the top half and 0 is left.

75. Alone — take away al — gives one.

76. You wouldn't grasp it.

77. You'd better get over it.

78. No, but I've seen a square dance.

79. It's a tall story (storey)....

80. I'd better not tell you— you might spread it around.

81. It hasn't ever been tolled (told)....

82. No, neither have I....

83. There's no tale to tell.

84. The rope wasn't tied to anything.

85. Fall off the bottom rung.

86. Don't give him any food.

87. By eating the sand which is there.

88. She had a crook with her.

89. By moving to another place.

90. When the T is taken away.

91. In a hambulance.

92. A stick of celery with high blood-pressure.

93. Use fourteen carats.

94. By gobblin.

95. With a seasaw.

96. Eat an entire peach and you'll immediately gain a stone.

97. Delighted.

98. It's something dat lures de fish.

99. Jump out of the way.

100. Take away the letter R.

101. Take the tobacco out.

102. They take short cuts.

103. Only one - after that it isn't empty!

104. Through its engineers.

105. Drive   down   the motorway. (Two whales = to Wales!)

106. I'll tell you later....

107. Make the trousers first.

108. 'Cos he's got 'E' on his pyjamas.

109. Say, 'Ready, teddy - go!'

110. By sparrowchute.

111. In a moo-seum.

112. Fully-armed.

113. By floor-lighting.

114. Drop him a line.

115. Cook him on Saturday.

116. Say 'one, two, flea - go!'

117. Two—an inside and an outside.

118. Put him in the front seat.

119. You can't. The bucket won't fit under it.

120. Dunno, but they start with hops.

121. Throw him off a cliff and he'll come down 'plump!'

122. Just one HUGE one!

123. Skinheads on a raft.

124. Condense it.

125. Somebody says, 'Ready, steady, glow!'

126. Knock over a full glass of milk.

127. Four: Tuesday, Thursday, today and tomorrow.
128. By public transport.
129. By his grave manner.
130. Look in the catalogue.
131. Rearrange the letters.
132. Sleep at night.
133. One P.
134. It came to him in a flash.
135. None. Pine trees don't have acorns.
136. Forty-six, the other six are only Lent.
137. B-L-N-D-P-G. A blind pig had no eyes.
138. By giving the bare facts.
139. All of them.
140. Bring a chair back with you.
141. Eleven. T-H-E-A-L-P-H-A-B-E-T.
142. Absolutely whacked.
143. Glue it to the floor.
144. Only four — calling a tail a leg doesn't make it one.
145. Sixteen: for better, for worse, for richer, for poorer.
146. Because it makes cream scream.
147. It won't run at all without winding.
148. Only once, because any later subtractions would not be from 160 but from a smaller number.
149. Take the spoon out of the cup.
150. Put it next to the wall.
151. Walk calmly to the next cage.
152. They throw them overboard and they wash ashore.
153. Bolt it down.
154. Sheik - to - sheik.
155. By going to his house when he isn't in.
156. Stick your finger in his eye.
157. He picked up his hammer and saw.
158. Push it.
159. Look at it in a mirror.
160. Well, have you ever seen a rabbit wearing spectacles?
161. You don't get down from an elephant; you get down from a duck.
162. It makes her hear.
163. He had an alarm clock.
164. When a pig is hungry he eats like a horse, and when a horse is hungry he eats like a pig.
165. Because it spits.
166. It's not easy to tell which witch is which.
167. He was shocked.
168. Read the label.
169. Under the letter N.
170. Hold it and then let go.
171. "Boo-hoo! Boo-hoo!"
172. Washington, D.C.
173. With sweeping gestures.
174. Take away the letter S.
175. With mountaineers.

176. "10Q." (Thank you) "You're welcome."
177. DK (decay).
178. U and I.
179. There must be a lot of ghost-to-ghost (coast-to-coast).
180. It starts coffin.
181. Run down.
182. It was burnt up.
183. His teacher told him to keep it to the grindstone.
184. He could feel it in his bones.
185. When you see eye-to-eye with yourself.
186. Because they always yell, "Tension!"
187. When it is a little pale (pail).
188. They both get paddled.
189. Take him to the North Pole.
190. Look for peanut shells.
191. With hush puppies.
192. A little swallow tells you.
193. It sounds off only when it is told (tolled).
194. The door won't shut.
195. By the footprints in the butter.
196. Frankly.
197. He said, "You really kill me."
198. Eat fortune cookies.
199. Throw water at him and he will let off steam.
200. Don't sleep long in it.
201. Ask someone else to break it.
202. Look for his Denmark (den mark).
203. With air breaks.
204. Because it was only a bluff.
205. Because they don't have to work.
206. Use a sundial.
207. Because when it rains it purrs (pours).
208. They use a harebrush (hairbrush).
209. Lengthen it.
210. XS (excess).
211. Delighted.
212. With a witch watch.
213. Perky.
214. Don't wind it.
215. Add 14 carrots (carats) to it.
216. Depressed.
217. Stick a finger in his eye.
218. When it is too heavy to lift.
219. Two in the front, two in the back, and one in the glove compartment.
220. A phew (few).
221. Drop it 4 feet. For the first 3 feet the egg will not hit anything.
222. If it's a three-dollar bill, you can be sure.
223. Like a kid.
224. Because Rome wasn't built in day.

225. None. A hole is empty.
226. A bit of water ends both of them.
227. Neither is right.
228. Twelve inchworms.
229. It depends on how many people are standing in it.
230. Because they are sure-footed.
231. A typewriter.
232. A fence.
233. A remark.
234. Dead.
235. Cork.
236. A scrapbook.
237. Fly past flea.
238. 3 minutes.
239. Time to get a new clock.
240. None—there are no 'f's in 'that'.
241. Glass....
242. A quarter to four.
243. Eleven, because the daughter is each son's sister.
244. Nine.
245. 9 minutes. (only 9 cuts are required).
246. 4 seconds - the interval between the strikes being 2 seconds each.
247. Myself.
248. Burple.
249. Waspberry jam.
250. Mistletoe. (Missal-toe!)

251. If an apple a day keeps the doctor away, what does a clove of garlic do?

252. If all the cars in Britain were pink, what would you have?

253. If a crocodile makes shoes what does a banana make?

254. If there are two tomatoes on a plate, which is the cowboy?

255. If twelve make a dozen how many make a million?

256. If you drop a white hat into the Red Sea, how does it come out?

257. If you put a crowd of Mastermind contestants in a London Underground train, what have you got?

258. If King Kong went to Hong Kong to play ping-pong and died, what would they put on his coffin?

259. If you saw a bird sitting on a twig, how could you get the twig without disturbing the bird?

260. If a ton of coal comes to $15, what will a ton of firewood come to?

261. If a boy ate his father and mother, what would that make him?

262. If a rooster laid a brown egg and a white egg, what kind of chicken would hatch?

263. If Harry's father is Bob's son, what relation is Harry to Bob?

264. If the green house is on the right side of the road, and the red house is on the left side of the road, where is the White House?

265. If an electric train travels 90 miles an hour in a westerly direction and the wind is blowing from the north, in which direction is the smoke blowing?

266. If cheese comes after dinner, what comes after cheese?
267. If thirteen birds were sitting on a telephone wire, and you shoot one, how many would be left?
268. If you are locked out of the house, how would you get in?
269. If an egg came floating down the Thames, where would it come from?
270. If a papa bull eats three bales of hay and a baby bull eats one bale, how much hay will a mama bull eat?
271. If two wrongs don't make a right, what did two rights make?
272. If you found a $5 note in every pocket of your coat, what would you have?
273. If your watch is broken, why can't you go fishing?
274. If a farmer raises wheat in dry weather, what does he raise in wet weather?
275. If the Forth Bridge were to collapse, what would they do?
276. If butter is 70p a pound in Oxford, what are window panes in Staffordshire?
277. If your are going for a hike in the desert, what should you carry?
278. If you were swimming in the Atlantic and an alligator attacked you, what would you do?
279. If a girl falls into a well, why can't her brother help her out?
280. If you fell downstairs, what would you fall against?
281. If five boys beat up one boy, what time would it be?
282. If you were walking in a jungle and met a lion, what time would it be?
283. If an African lion fought an African tiger, who would win?
284. If a doctor fell into a well, what should he have done instead?
285. If a band plays in a thunderstorm, who is most likely to get hit by lightning?
286. If the Prime Minister went to the circus and a lion ate him, what time would it be?
287. If you throw a pumpkin in the air, what comes down?
288. If you cross a cat and a pickle, what do you have?

289. If we breathe oxygen in the daytime, what do we breathe at night?

290. If you dropped a tomato on your toe, would it hurt much?

291. If there were ten cats in a boat and one jumped out, how many would be left?

292. If you add 2-forget and 2-forget, what do you get?

293. If you cross a bee and chopped meat, what do you get?

294. If you put three ducks in a carton, what do you get?

295. If April showers bring May flowers, what do the May flowers bring?

296. If you had 5 potatoes and had to divide them qually between 3 people, what should you do?

297. If a boy is spanked by his mother and his father, who hurts the most?

298. If you take half from a half dollar, what do you have?

299. If the ruler of Russia was called the Czar and his wife the Czarina, what were his children called?

300. If you don't feel well, what do you probably have?

301. In what way are the letter "A" and noon the same?

302. In a certain city there is a corner with four stores. One is a bakery, one a candy store, one a drug store, and one a book store. Outside the drug store is a policeman. Why is the policeman called Oscar?

303. Is it better to say, "The yolk of an egg is white," or "The yolk of an egg are white?"

304. In what liquid does the Queen take her medicine?

305. In what month do people eat the least?

306. In a fight between a hedgehog and a fox, who won?

307. Is it possible for a man to marry his widow's sister?

308. Is censorship a good thing or not?

309. Is it possible to drop an egg on to a concrete floor without even denting it?

310. Is it dangerous to swim on a full stomach?

311. Is life worth living?

312. Is it safe to write a letter on an empty stomach?

313. 'Look, there's a nail!' 'Where?'

314. Little Nancy Etticoat,
     In a white petticoat
     And a red nose,
     The longer she stands
     The shorter she grows
     Who is she?

315. Luck had it first, Paul had it last; boys never have it; girls have it but once; Miss Polly had it twice in the same place, but when she married Peter Jones she never had it again.

316. Make one word from the letters in New Door.

317. Mrs. Bigger had a baby. Who was bigger?

318. My first means equality; my second inferiority; and my whole superiority.

319. My mother has only 2 children, but her son is not my brother. Who is he?

320. Name a shooting star.

321. Name the rudest of all birds.

322. Now you see it, now you don't—what is it?

323. On which side of Jack Trot's house did his Beanstalk grow?

324. On which side of a country church is the graveyard always situated?

325. On what side of a school does an elm tree grow?

326. On the way to a water hole a zebra met 6 giraffes. Each giraffe had 3 monkeys hanging from its neck. Each monkey had 2 birds on its tail. How many animals were going to the water hole?

327. On which side does a chicken have most feathers?

328. On what kind of ships do students study?

329. On what nuts can pictures hang?

330. Press me at the bottom and meet me on the top. Who am I?

331. Pray tell me,
     ladies, if you can,
     who is that highly favoured man,
     who though he's married many a wife,
     may yet be single all his life?

332. Purple, yellow, red and green,
     All the colours in between
     The King cannot reach it, or the queen -
     Or any man whose power is great.
     I bow before rain
     Tell me this riddle before I count eight!

333. Soldiers mark time with their feet. What does the same
     thing with its hands?

334. Some ducks were walking down a path. There was a duck
     in front of two ducks, a duck behind two ducks, and a
     duck between two ducks. How many ducks in all?

335. Spell extra wise in two letters?

336. Spell expediency in 5 letters.

337. Spell electricity with three letters.

338. Spell "pound" in two letters.

339. Spell Indian tent with two letters.

340. Take 2 apples from 3 apples. How many have you got?

341. The Bible tells us the colours of the winds and storms.
     What are they?

342. The brother-in-law of my mother's only brother is closely
     related to me. Who is he?

343. The alphabet goes from A to Z. What goes from Z to A?

344. Three girls stood under an umbrella but none of them got
     wet. Why?

345. There was a girl in our town,
     Silk an' satin was her gown
     Silk an' satin, gold an' velvet;
     Guess her name, three times I've telled it.

346. The more there is of it, the less you see. What is it?

347. To whom does every man take off his hat?

348. To what question can you answer nothing but 'yes'?

349. To whom did Paul Revere give his handkerchief?

350. Two men dig a hole in five days. How many days would it
     take them to dig half a hole?

351. Two baseball teams played a game; one team won, but no
     man touched a base. How could that be?

352. Two mothers and two daughters went to a football match. There were only three seats available. They took them and all sat down. How was that possible?

353. Two duellists were standing a foot apart—one facing east and the other west. How could they shoot at each other without turning round?

354. We all know that a nun rolling down a hill goes black-and-white-and-black-and-white, but what is black-and-white-and goes ha-ha?

355. Where was King Solomon's Temple?

356. We travel much, yet prisoners are,
     And close confined to boot;
     We with the swiftest horse keep pace,
     Yet always go on foot?

357. With what do you fill a bucket to make it lighter than when empty?

358. With what vegetable do you throw away the outside, cook the inside, eat the outside, and throw away the inside.

359. What is the capital of Lapland?

360. What has large antlers and wears white gloves?

361. What is a zebra?

362. What's the best year for kangaroos?

363. What's blue and yellow and has a wing span of 14 metres?

364. What do you give a pig with a sore nose?

365. What are spider's webs good for?

366. What wobbles when it flies?

367. What word of five letters is left with one, if two are removed, and two, if only one is removed?

368. What do you find in Quality Street?

369. What goes zzub-zzub?

370. What's white and goes up?

371. What do you call a cat who swallowed a duck?

372. What is the noisiest of all games?

373. What did the big candle say to the little candle?

374. What turns without moving?

375. What room has no walls, floor, ceiling or window?
376. What do you do with a sick budgie?
377. What nut has no shell?
378. What is the hardest thing about learning to ride a bike?
379. What are hot, greasy and romantic?
380. What must you know to be an auctioneer?
381. What would you do with a sick wasp?
382. What is the opposite of cock-a-doodle-do?
383. What is the biggest moth of all?
384. What are hippies for?
385. What note do you get if an elephant playing the piano falls down a mine shaft?
386. What did the balloon say to the pin?
387. What is it that's got meat in it, also bread and tomatoes, and orange, is tied up in cellophane and flies through belfries?
388. What do cornflakes wear on their feet?
389. What does an elephant do when it rains?
390. What has a bottom at the top?
391. What is the invention that enables you to see through the thickest walls?
392. What language do they speak in Cuba?
393. What is the hottest letter of the alphabet?
394. What is it that goes 99 plonk?
395. What did the necklace say to the hat?
396. What did one rose say to the other rose?
397. What has four legs and can't walk?
398. What is the longest night of the year?
399. What does one witch say to another witch?
400. What orders does everyone like to receive?
401. What is the longest word in the English language?
402. What is a sailor who is married with seven children called?
403. What is it that's yellow and very dangerous?
404. What goes up a drainpipe down, but can't go down a drainpipe up?

405. What did the toothpaste say to the brush?

406. What happens to cows after an earthquake?

407. What's brown and can see just as well from either end?

408. What is it you can put in your right hand but not in your left?

409. What did the envelope say to the stamp?

410. What has a neck but no head?

411. What did the pig say when the chef cut off his tail?

412. What did the drunken chicken lay?

413. What's round and bad-tempered?

414. What did the jack say to the car?

415. What do lady sheep wear?

416. What is always behind time?

417. What's mad and goes to the moon?

418. What has four legs and one foot?

419. What flour do elves use?

420. What did Rome-o?

421. What has a bed but does not sleep? What has a mouth but does not speak?

422. What is a happy tin in the United States?

423. What did one eye say to the other eye?

424. What is the definition of a harp?

425. What trees do fingers and thumbs grow on?

426. What walks on its head all day?

427. What did the carpet say to the floor?

428. What do cannibals have for lunch?

429. What does the sea say to the sand?

430. What is long, has a brown hat and lies in a box?

431. What can you give someone and still keep?

432. What can you touch, see and make but can't hold?

433. What animals need oiling?

434. What's black when clean and white when dirty?

435. What letters are not in the alphabet?

436. What is the similarity between soldiers and dentists?

437. What coat do you put on only when it's wet?

438. What is a calf after it is one year old?

439. What runs but has no legs?

440. What does a deaf fisherman need?

441. What tongue never speaks?

442. What is worse than a giraffe with a sore neck?

443. What is hail?

444. What did the paper say to the pencil?

445. What is the difference between a teacher and an engine driver?

446. What did one telephone say to another?

447. What is the difference between Prince Charles and a football?

448. What did one wall say to the other?

449. What is the difference between a soldier and a lady?

450. What happens when you are mean to a jigsaw puzzle?

451. What has a head and a tail, but no body?

452. What word is made shorter by lengthening it?

453. What brings Australian bats out in broad daylight?

454. What is the only sport where the winners move backwards?

455. What kind of table do we cook and eat?

456. What is it that occurs once in every minute, twice in moment, and not once in a year?

457. What is the difference between weather which is slightly foggy and a gentleman?

458. What is the difference between a frightened child and a shipwrecked sailor?

459. What kind of pets do we sometimes eat?

460. What is smaller than the mouth of the smallest worm?

461. What can you knit without knitting needles?

462. What is the difference between a jail and a man who deals in watches?

463. What shape is a kiss?

464. What is it that never asks questions, but has to be continuously answered?

465. What did Adam and Eve do when they were turned out of the Garden of Eden?

466. What is it that nobody wants, but nobody wants to lose?

467. What did William Tell Junior say when his father shot the apple?

468. What is the difference between a woman who gossips and a looking glass?

469. What is it that is purchased by the yard and worn by the foot?

470. What vegetable is dangerous if found on board a ship?

471. What is the difference between a lazy schoolboy and an angler?

472. What kind of a fall makes you unconscious, but doesn't hurt you?

473. What is nothing but holes tied to holes, but as strong as iron?

474. What always tastes hot and has ice in it?

475. What happened to the man who listened to a match?

476. What is it that men do standing up, ladies do sitting down and dogs on three legs?

477. What would you call five bottles of fizzy lemonade?

478. What wears a coat all winter and pants in the summer?

479. What is cowhide most used for?

480. What water won't freeze?

481. What do you call an American drawing?

482. What is grey and has four legs and a trunk?

483. What did Dick Turpin say at the end of his ride to York?

484. What did Mrs. Spider say when she broke a new web?

485. What did the policeman say to the three-headed man?

486. What did the mayonnaise say to the fridge?

487. What do you call a bald-headed smiler?

488. What do you take off last when you get into bed?

489. What did the crook who stole the calendar get?

490. What did the pilot say as he left the pub?
491. What training do you need to be a rubbish collector?
492. What do we do with trees after we chop them down?
493. What happened to the man who couldn't tell porridge from putty?
494. What is green and hairy and goes up and down?
495. What were Tarzan's last words?
496. What is the opposite of minimum?
497. What do you call a constipated budgie?
498. What do you call an Eskimo wearing five balaclavas and a crash helmet?
499. What has four legs, a tail, whiskers and flies?
500. What did the German say to the broken clock?

Answers

251. Keeps everyone away!
252. A car-nation.
253. Slippers.
254. Neither—they're both redskins.
255. Very few.
256. Wet.
257. A Tube of Smarties.
258. A lid.
259. Wait until the bird flew away.
260. Ashes.
261. An orphan.
262. None. Roosters don't lay eggs.
263. Bob is Harry's grandfather.
264. In Washington, U.S.A.
265. There is no smoke from an electric train.
266. A mouse.
267. None. They would fly away.
268. Sing until you get the right key.
269. From a chicken.
270. Nothing. There is no such thing as a mama bull.
271. An aeroplane.
272. Someone else's coat.
273. Because you haven't the time.
274. An umbrella.
275. Build a fifth.
276. Glass.
277. A thirst-aid kit.
278. Nothing. There are no alligators in the Atlantic.
279. Because he cannot be a brother and assist her too.
280. Against your will.

281. Five to one.
282. Time to run.
283. Neither. There are no tigers in Africa.
284. Attended to the sick, and left the well alone.
285. The conductor.
286. Ate P.M.
287. Squash.
288. A picklepuss.
289. Nitrogen.
290. Yes, if it were in a can.
291. None, because they were all copycats.
292. 4-gotten.
293. A humburger.
294. A box of quackers.
295. Pilgrims.
296. Mash them first.
297. The boy.
298. A dollar.
299. Sardines.
300. A pair of gloves on your hands.
301. Both are in the middle of day.
302. Because that is his name.
303. Neither. An egg yolk is yellow.
304. Inside her (Cider).
305. February—it's the shortest month.
306. The hedgehog won on points.
307. No—he'd be dead.
308. It depends on whether the result makes censor not.
309. Yes, it is not easy to dent concrete.
310. Yes, it is better to swim in water.
311. It depends on the liver.
312. Quite safe, but better to write on paper.
313. 'On the end of my finger!'
314. A candle.
315. The letter L.
316. One word.
317. The baby, because it was a little bigger.
318. Match-less.
319. Myself—the other child is a girl.
320. Clint Eastwood.
321. The mockingbird.
322. A black cat walking over a zebra crossing.
323. On the outside.
324. The outside.
325. On the outside
326. Only the zebra. The others were coming away from it.
327. On the outside.
328. Scholarships.
329. Walnuts.
330. Toothpaste.
331. A clergyman.
332. A rainbow.
333. A watch.
334. Three ducks, waddling single file.
335. YY (2y's).
336. XPDNC
337. NRG (energy)

338. Lb.
339. TP.
340. 2 of course.
341. It says, 'The wind rose and the storms blew (blue)'.
342. My father.
343. Zebra.
344. It wasn't raining.
345. Anne.
346. Darkness.
347. His barber.
348. What does YES spell?
349. To the town crier.
350. None. You can't dig half a hole.
351. It was a woman's team.
352. There were only 3— grandmother, mother and daughter.
353. They were already facing each other.
354. The nun that pushed her!
355. In his forehead.
356. Spurs.
357. Holes.
358. Corn on the cob.
359. The letter L.
360. Mickey Moose.
361. A horse behind bars.
362. The leap year.
363. A two and a half ton budgie.
364. Oinkment.
365. Spiders.
366. A Jellycopter.
367. Stone - St - one.
368. Chocolates.

369. A bee flying backwards.
370. A stupid snowflake.
371. A duck-filled fatty puss.
372. Tennis, because you can't play it without raising a racket.
373. "Going out tonight?"
374. Milk - when it turns sour.
375. A mushroom.
376. Give him tweetment.
377. A doughnut.
378. The pavement.
379. Chips that pass in the night.
380. Lots.
381. Take it to waspital.
382. Cock-a-doodle-don't.
383. A mam-moth.
384. To keep your leggies up.
385. A Flat miner (A flat minor)
386. 'Hi, buster!'
387. The Lunchpack of Notre Dame.
388. K-logs (clogs).
389. Gets wet.
390. A leg.
391. A window.
392. Cubic.
393. B, because it makes oil boil.
394. A centipede with a wooden leg.
395. You go on ahead - I'll hang around.
396. "Hiya, Bud".
397. Two pairs of trousers.
398. A fortnight.

399. 'Snap, cackle and pop!'

400. Postal orders.

401. Smiles - because there's a mile between its first and last letters.

402. Daddy.

403. Shark-infested custard.

404. An umbrella.

405. Give me a squeeze and I'll meet you outside the tube.

406. They give milk shakes.

407. A horse with his eyes shut.

408. Your left elbow.

409. 'Stick with me, baby, and we'll go places!'

410. A bottle.

411. 'This is the end of me....'

412. Scotch eggs.

413. A vicious circle.

414. 'Can I give you a lift?'

415. Ewe-niforms.

416. The back of a clock.

417. A loony module.

418. A bed.

419. Elf-raising flour.

420. For what Juli-et.

421. A river.

422. A-merry-can.

423. Something's come between us that smells.

424. A nude piano.

425. Palm trees.

426. A drawing-pin stuck in your shoe.

427. I've got you covered.

428. Baked beings.

429. Nothing - it waves.

430. A match.

431. Your word.

432. A shadow.

433. Mice, because they squeak.

434. A blackboard.

435. Those that are in the postbox.

436. They both have to drill.

437. A coat of paint.

438. A two-year-old calf.

439. A tap.

440. A herring-aid.

441. The tongue in your shoe.

442. A centipede with corns.

443. Hard-boiled rain.

444. Now I have caught the point.

445. One trains the mind and the other minds the train.

446. Let's get engaged.

447. Charles is heir to the throne and a football is thrown into the air.

448. I'll meet you at the corner.

449. One faces the powder and the other powders the face.

450. It goes to pieces.

451. A coin.

452. Short.

453. The cricket season.

454. Tug-of-war.

455. Vegetables.

456. The letter M.

457. One is a mist and the other a mister.
458. One clings to his Ma and the other to his Spar (his Pa).
459. Crumpets.
460. The things it eats.
461. Your brows.
462. One watches cells and the other cells (sells) watches.
463. Elliptical (a lip tickle).
464. The doorbell.
465. They raised Cain.
466. A law suit.
467. That's an arrow escape.
468. One speaks without reflecting, and the other reflects without speaking.
469. Carpet.
470. A leek (leak).
471. One hates his books and the other baits his hooks.
472. Falling asleep.
473. A link-chain.
474. Spice.
475. He burnt his ear.
476. Shake hands.

477. A pop group.
478. A dog.
479. Holding cows together.
480. Boiling water.
481. A Yankee Doodle.
482. A mouse going on a holiday.
483. Whoooaaa!
484. Darn it!
485. 'Allo', 'allo', 'allo!'
486. 'Close the door—I'm dressing.
487. Yull Grynner.
488. Your feet off the floor.
489. Twelve months.
490. Must fly now!
491. None, you pick it up as you go along.
492. Chop them up.
493. All his windows fell out.
494. A gooseberry in a lift.
495. Who greased the vine?
496. Minidad
497. Chirrup of figs.
498. Anything you like - he can't hear a thing
499. A dead cat.
500. 'Ve half vays off making you tock!'

501. What would you see at a chicken show?
502. What goes black and white and black and white and black and white and black and white...?
503. What happened when a man bought a paper shop?
504. What do Frenchmen eat for breakfast?
505. What do cannibals eat for breakfast?
506. What is brown, has four feet, a hump and is found in Alaska?
507. What does the winner of a running-race always lose?
508. What's shut when it's open and open when it's shut?
509. What should you do for a starving cannibal?
510. What happens if pigs fly?
511. What nut sounds like a sneeze?
512. What did one tomato say to the other?
513. What has one hundred limbs but cannot walk?
514. What tools do we use in arithmetic?
515. What gets wetter as it dries?
516. What is striped and goes round and round?
517. What's stupid and yellow?
518. What dance do ducks prefer?
519. What party game did Jekyll like best?
520. What do you call an astronaut's watch?
521. What did the Father Phone say to his son?
522. What is a waste of energy?
523. What time did the Chinaman go to the dentist?
524. What's big and yellow and eats rocks?
525. What is the largest mouse in the world?

526. What lies at the bottom of the sea and shivers?

527. What kind of meringues repeat?

528. What happened when the axe fell on the car?

529. What is hairy and coughs?

530. What's green and holds up a stage coach?

531. What was purple and wanted to rule the world?

532. What do you get if you run over a canary with a lawn-mower?

533. What did the rock pool say to another rock pool?

534. What is yellow and has twenty-two legs?

535. What insect is musical?

536. What are frogs' favourite tales?

537. What goes in pink and comes out blue?

538. What did the Daddy Hedgehog say to his son as he was about to spank him?

539. What did the spider say to the beetle?

540. What did the picture say to the wall?

541. What did Cinderella say when the chemist mislaid her photographs?

542. What do you call someone who has a dictionary in his Wellies?

543. What is a common illness in China?

544. What do jelly bodies wear on their feet?

545. What do ducks like on television?

546. What goes A B C D E F G H I J K L M N O P Q R S T U V W X Y Z slurp?

547. What has one horn and gives milk?

548. What is pretty, has big teeth and flies?

549. What do you get if you dial 49834467235574639283746 2?

550. What do you get if you pour boiling water down a rabbit hole?

551. What travels 100 miles per hour underground?

552. What's worse than raining cats and dogs?

553. What noise does a cat make on the motorway?

554. What was Nelson's baby brother called?

555. What goes dot-dot-croak, croak-dot-croak, dot-croak-dot-croak?
556. What goes in black and comes out white?
557. What's seven feet high, green and sits in the corner?
558. What was Noah's profession?
559. What do you call a baby whale?
560. What did the blackbird say to the scarecrow?
561. What goes cluck-cluck bang?
562. What did the pink panther say when he stepped on the ant?
563. What did one Egyptian say to the other Egyptian?
564. What is woolly, covered in chocolate and goes round the sun?
565. What did the strawberry say to the second strawberry?
566. What dog has no tail?
567. What does a ball do when it stops rolling?
568. What game do horses like?
569. What swings through trees and is very dangerous?
570. What do you get when you jump in the Red Sea?
571. What's black and white and red all over?
572. What was the police dog's telephone number?
573. What did the German policeman say to his chest?
574. What do you call a foreign body in a chip pan?
575. What do you get if a cat swallows a ball of wool?
576. What is yellow, has twenty-two legs and goes to church?
577. What lives under the sea and carries 64 people?
578. What did the cork say to the bottle?
579. What's the best way to catch a squirrel?
580. What's brown and white and yellow and goes at 125 miles per hour?
581. What did the puddle say to the rain?
582. What did the invisible man say to his girlfriend?
583. What do you do if you split your sides laughing?
584. What do spacemen play in their spare time?

585. What do mermaids eat for breakfast?
586. What did the plug say to the wall?
587. What's yellow on the inside and green on the outside?
588. What goes tick-tick woof-woof?
589. What goes ha-ha-ha clonk?
590. What do you get when you eat foam?
591. What is the worst kind of weather for rats and mice?
592. What is a clock?
593. What did Batman's mother say when she wanted to call him for lunch?
594. What did the Lone Ranger say when he went to the refuse tip?
595. What is red, has bumps and a horse and lives on the prairie?
596. What must you be careful not to do when it's raining cats and dogs?
597. What do you call a 400 kilogram grizzly bear with a bad temper?
598. What is the most common illness in birds?
599. What can't you do if you put 250 melons in the fridge?
600. What happened to the plastic surgeon when he stood by the fire?
601. What exams are horses good at?
602. What is yellow and flickers?
603. What cakes do children dislike?
604. What is a buttress?
605. What's the best place to go to when you're dying?
606. What is bought by the yard and worn by the foot?
607. What did one toe say to the next toe?
608. What did the digital watch say to her mother?
609. What happened to the man who jumped off a bridge in Paris?
610. What travels round the world yet stays in one corner?
611. What flashes by but doesn't move?
612. What is full of holes but can hold water?

613. What happens to the girl who misses the school bus?
614. What makes the Tower of Pisa lean?
615. What is open when it's closed and closed when it's open?
616. What is it that even the most careful person overlooks?
617. What runs and whistles but can't talk?
618. What is a tornado?
619. What is the longest word in the dictionary?
620. What am I if someone takes away all my letters?
621. What is the best place for a party on board ship?
622. What should you do if your nose goes on strike?
623. What is the best way to cover a cushion?
624. What did the idiot do with a flea in his ear?
625. What can never be made right?
626. What vegetable do you need a plumber for?
627. What has four eyes and a mouth?
628. What is a sausage dog?
629. What is yellow, soft and goes round and round?
630. What food is impertinent?
631. What did Lot do when his wife turned into a pillar of salt?
632. What did the French chef do when a customer fainted?
633. What do you get in Friday paper?
634. What bow can't you tie?
635. What is the fastest vegetable in the world?
636. What is purple and 4,000 miles long?
637. What clothes do lawyers wear in court?
638. What did the man say when he stepped on a choc bar?
639. What will happen to you at Christmas?
640. What's rich and goes putt-putt?
641. What would you say to a German barber?
642. What do you always take down when you're run over by a car?
643. What two kinds of fish are needed to make a shoe?
644. What key went to University?
645. What tune do you sing in a car?

646. What did the bell say when it fell into the water?
647. What athlete is the warmest in winter?
648. What travels faster: heat or cold?
649. What fish do dogs chase?
650. What doesn't ask questions but must always be answered?
651. What do you call a letter when it's dropped down the chimney?
652. What nail can't you hit with a hammer?
653. What is the softest bed a baby can sleep on?
654. What is the principal part of a lion called?
655. What driver can't drive?
656. What jam can't you put on your bread?
657. What runs round a garden without moving?
658. What do misers do when it's cold?
659. What can you make that can't be seen?
660. What is a container that hasn't any hinges but inside has a golden treasure?
661. What whistles when it's hot?
662. What are the best things to put in an apple pie?
663. What's the biggest nut in the British Army?
664. What happens if you walk under a cow?
665. What gets bigger the more you take away?
666. What kind of lights did Noah have on the ark?
667. What do you call an Irish spider?
668. What is a cow that eats grass?
669. What is the shortest bridge in the world?
670. What kind of umbrella does a Russian carry when it's raining?
671. What is a volcano?
672. What is the definition of a minimum?
673. What is the smallest ant in the world?
674. What is big, has four wheels and flies?
675. What did the guests sing at the Eskimo's coming-of-age?
676. What will a wise man say on the Last Day?

677. What did Mrs. Christmas say to her husband during the storm?

678. What is black and white and eight wheels?

679. What happened to the idiot who sat on the floor?

680. What has a horn and drives?

681. What do Eskimos use for money?

682. What kinds of cans are there in Mexico?

683. What's a good place for water-skiing?

684. What pop group kills household germs?

685. What do miners play in the pit?

686. What does a pig use to write his letters with?

687. What vegetable plays snooker?

688. What soup do Irish cannibals like best?

689. What is Shakespeare's most popular play in the Orient?

690. What is Father Christmas's wife called?

691. What is a mermaid?

692. What lives in a pod and is a Kung Fu expert?

693. What's big, hairy and can fly?

694. What do cannibal children like playing best?

695. What do you get if you give sugar and egg-whites to a monkey?

696. What's yellow and goes round and round?

697. What happened to the man who slept with his head under the pillow?

698. What's black and white and extremely difficult?

699. What's green and white and bounces?

700. What's white and climbs trees?

701. What's white and blue and climbs trees?

702. What is yellow and goes click-click?

703. What did Queen Guinevere say when she fell in love?

704. What did Tarzan say when the tiger started chewing on his leg?

705. What drink do jungle big cats prefer?

706. What kind of warmth do sheep enjoy in wives?

707. What did the policeman have in his sandwiches?

708. What was Beethoven's favourite fruit? (Sing to the opening four notes of Beethoven's Fifth Symphony):

709. What do you call a potato that insults the farmer?

710. What do m ɜers do when it's very cold?

711. What happened to the man who dreamed he was eating a giant marshmallow?

712. What is the crocodile's favourite game?

713. What did the man say when he found he was going bald?

714. What kind of bird is always around when there's something to eat or drink?

715. What's in the church, but not the steeple, the Parson has it, but not the people.

716. What is the difference between a bell and a cook?

717. What can run but can't walk?

718. What does an artist like best to draw?

719. What has a head, can't think, but drives?

720. What musical key makes a good army officer?

721. What animal goes to sleep with its shoes on?

722. What has six legs, but only walks with four?

723. What kind of tunes do we enjoy most?

724. What river is ever without a beginning and ending?

725. What goes all the way from Lands' End to John o'Groats without moving?

726. What didn't Adam and Eve have that everyone in the world has had?

727. What question can never be answered by 'Yes'?

728. What are the warmest months of the year?

729. What animal eats and drinks with its tail?

730. What 'bus' crossed the ocean?

731. What wears shoes, but has no feet?

732. What animal keeps the best time?

733. What lands as often on its tail as it does on its head?

734. What did one flea say to the other flea?

735. What does a beard do for a man who seldom tells the truth?

736. What does everyone have that he can always count on?
737. What is the hardest thing about learning to roller-skate?
738. What is the best way to eat spaghetti?
739. What has four legs and flies?
740. What herb cures all diseases?
741. What runs around all day and then lies under the bed with its tongue hanging out?
742. What is it that increases the more it is shared with others?
743. What is black and white and red all over?
744. What did the mother strawberry say to the baby strawberry?
745. What is the difference between a thunderclap and a lion with a toothache?
746. What did the judge say when he got home after work?
747. What are the three easiest ways to spread rumour?
748. What is the difference between a doormat and a bottle of medicine?
749. What is the reddest side of an apple?
750. What has a foot at each end and a foot in the middle?

Answers

501. Hentertainment.
502. A penguin rolling down a hill.
503. It blew away.
504. Huit heures bix.
505. Buttered host.
506. A lost camel.
507. His breath.
508. A level-crossing.
509. Give him a hand.
510. Bacon goes up.
511. A cashoo!
512. You go ahead and I'll ketchup.
513. A tree.
514. Multipliers.
515. A towel.
516. A zebra in a revolving door.
517. Thick custard.
518. A quackstep.
519. Hyde and seek.
520. A luna-tick.
521. You're too young to be engaged.
522. Telling a hair-raising story to a bald man!
523. Two-thirty. (Tooth hurtee)

524. A big yellow rock-eater.
525. A hippopota-mouse.
526. A nervous wreck.
527. Boo-meringues.
528. There was an axe-i-dent.
529. A coconut with a cold.
530. Dick Gherkin.
531. Alexander the Grape.
532. Shredded tweet.
533. 'Show us your mussels'.
534. Banana United.
535. A humbug.
536. Croak and dagger stories.
537. A swimmer on a cold day.
538. 'This is going to hurt me far more than it will you....'
539. Stop bugging me.'
540. 'I've got you covered.'
541. 'Some day my prints will come.'
542. Smarty-boots.
543. Kung Flu.
544. Gum boots.
545. Duckmetaries.
546. A man eating alphabet soup.
547. A milk delivery van.
548. A killer butterfly.
549. A blister on your finger.
550. Hot Cross Bunnies.
551. A mole on a motor-bike.
552. Hailing taxis.
553. MAAIIIOWWWW!
554. Half-Nelson.
555. Morse toad.
556. A miller's boot.

557. The Incredible Sulk.
558. He was an Ark-itect.
559. A little squirt.
560. 'I'll knock the stuffing out of you'.
561. A chicken in a minefield.
562. (Sing 'Pink Panther tune') 'Dead - ant, dead - ant, dead - ant,....
563. 'I can't remember your name but your fez is familiar.'
564. A Mars Baaaa!
565. 'However did we get into this jam?'
566. A hotdog.
567. Looks around.
568. Stable-tennis.
569. A chimpanzee with a machine-gun.
570. Wet.
571. A sun-burnt penguin.
572. Canine, canine, canine.
573. 'You're under a-vest!'
574. An Unidentified Frying Object.'
575. Mittens.
576. A Chinese football team.
577. An octobus.
578. 'If you don't behave I'll plug you'.
579. Hang upside own from a tree and look like a nut.
580. A train-driver's egg sandwich.
581. 'Drop in sometime.'
582. 'Baby, you're outta sight!'
583. Run till you get a stitch.

584. Astronaughtsand crosses.
585. Merma-lade on toast.
586. 'Socket to me, baby!'
587. A banana disguised as a cucumber.
588. A watch dog.
589. A man laughing his head off.
590. Soft in the head.
591. When it's raining cats and dogs.
592. The mating call of a Chinese frog.
593. (Sing) 'Dinner-dinner dinner, dinner dinner..., BATMAN!
594. 'To-de-dump, to-de-dump, to-de-dump, to-de-dump....'
595. The Lone Raspberry.
596. Step in a poodle.
597. Sir.
598. Flu.
599. Shut the door.
600. He melted.
601. Hay levels.
602. A lemon with a loose connection.
603. Cakes of soap.
604. A female goat
605. The living room.
606. A blubber mouth.
607. Don't look now but there's a big heel following us.
608. 'Look, Ma! No hands!'
609. He went in Seine.
610. A postage stamp.
611. A telegraph pole when you're traveling in a car.
612. A sponge.
613. She catches it when she gets home.
614. It doesn't eat much.
615. Tower Bridge.
616. His nose.
617. A railway train.
618. Mother Nature doing the twist.
619. Elastic, because it stretches.
620. A postman who's been mugged.
621. Where the funnel be.
622. Picket.
623. Sit on it.
624. He shot it.
625. Your left ear.
626. A leek!
627. The Mississippi.
628. A hot dog with no bread.
629. A long-playing omelette.
630. Sauce.
631. He put her in the cellar.
632. Gave her the quiche of life.
633. Fish and chips. (Fri-day)
634. A rainbow.
635. A runner bean!
636. The Grape Wall of China
637. Lawsuits.
638. 'I've set foot on Mars!'
639. Yule be happy.
640. A sunburned golf-pro.
641. 'Good morning, Herr Dresser!'
642. Its registration number.
643. A sole and an eel.

644. A Yale.
645. A car-toon.
646. 'I'm (w)ringing wet!'
647. The long jumper.
648. Heat, because it's easy to catch a cold.
649. Catfish.
650. A telephone.
651. Blackmail.
652. Your fingernail.
653. Cot-on wool.
654. Its mane.
655. A screwdriver.
656. Traffic jam.
657. A fence.
658. Sit round a candle.
659. A noise.
660. An egg.
661. A kettle.
662. Your teeth!
663. The kernel.
664. You get a pat on the head.
665. A hole.
666. Floodlights.
667. Paddy Longlegs.
668. A lawn-mooer.
669. The bridge of your nose.
670. A wet one!
671. A mountain with hiccups.
672. A woman with only one child.
673. An infant.
674. A rubbish cart.
675. 'Freeze A Jolly Good Fellow....'
676. 'Armageddon out of here....'

677. 'Come and look at the reindeer.'
678. A nun on roller skates.
679. She fell off.
680. A car.
681. Ice lolly.
682. Mexicans.
683. A sloping lake.
684. The Bleach Boys.
685. Mine-opoly.
686. Pen and ink.
687. A cue-cumber.
688. The birth of a boy.
689. Asia Like It.
690. Mrs Christmas.
691. A deep-she fish.
692. Bruce Pea.
693. King Kongcorde.
694. Swallow my leader.
695. Meringue Outan.
696. A banana in a washing machine.
697. When he woke up he found the fairies had taken all his teeth out.
698. An A-level exam paper.
699. A spring onion.
700. A fridge. I lied about it climbing trees.
701. A fridge wearing denims. (And I'm still lying about it climbing trees).
702. A ball-point banana.
703. 'Arthur any more at home like you?'
704. AAAAAAAAAAAAAAAAAA! (Give the Tarzan yell)
705. Lyons' quick brew.

706. Central bleating.
707. Traffic jam.
708. Eanana-nanaa!
709. A fresh vegetable.
710. Light it.
711. When he woke up his pillow had disappeared.
712. Snap.
713. Hair today, gone tomorrow.
714. A swallow.
715. The letter R.
716. One makes a din, the other a dinner.
717. Water.
718. His wages.
719. A hammer.
720. A sharp major.
721. A horse
722. A horse with a rider.
723. For-tunes.
724. S-ever-N.
725. The road.
726. Parents.
727. 'Are you asleep?'
728. September, November and December, because they all have embers in them.
729. All of them. They don't remove their tails for eating and drinking.
730. Columbus.
731. The pavement.
732. A watchdog.
733. A penny.
734. 'Shall we walk or shall we take the dog?'
735. It keeps him from being a bare-faced liar.
736. His fingers.
737. The ground.
738. First, open your mouth.
739. A dead horse.
740. Thyme.
741. Your shoe.
742. Happiness.
743. A newspaper.
744. Don't get into a jam.
745. One pours with rain and the roars with pain.
746. It's been another trying day.
747. Telephone, telegraph - and tell a gossip.
748. One is taken up and shaken, the other is shaken up and taken.
749. The outside.
750. A yardstick.

Riddles 751-1000

751. What do all ships weigh, regardless of size?

752. What kind of house weighs the least?

753. What often falls but never gets hurt?

754. What happened when the steam hammer was invented?

755. What is it that everyone needs, everyone gives, everyone asks for and very few take?

756. What goes farther the slower it goes?

757. What often falls but never gets hurt?

758. What is it that the man who makes it does not need, the man who buys it does not use for himself, and the person who uses it does so without knowing?

759. What is it a girl looks for but hopes she won't find?

760. What is pronounced like one letter, written with three letters, and belongs to all animals?

761. What did the Eskimo say when he'd built his igloo?

762. What is lengthened by a cut at both ends?

763. What kind of robbery is the easiest?

764. What did the burglar say to the lady who caught him stealing her silver?

765. What does a garden say when it laughs?

766. What grows larger the more you take away?

767. What is filled every morning and emptied every night, except once a year when it is filled at night and emptied in the morning?

768. What is easy to get into but hard to get out of?

769. What is better than presence of mind in a road accident?

770. What's the easiest way to get on TV?

771. What happened when the Eskimo girl fell out with her boyfriend?
772. What is boiled, then cooled, sweetened then soured?
773. What happened to the boy who ran away with the circus?
774. What does a hard-working gardener always grow?
775. What is another name for a butcher's boy?
776. What should we do instead of complaining when it rains?
777. What is the difference between a glass of water and a glass of whisky?
778. What did one angel say to the other angel?
779. What gets harder to catch the faster you run?
780. What can be measured, but has no length, width or thickness?
781. What is the animal with the highest intelligence?
782. What's the best place for a motorist to get a nice 'cuppa'?
783. What did the windshield wiper say to the other windshield wiper?
784. What turns everything round but doesn't move?
785. What is the longest view in the world?
786. What word of three syllables contains twenty-six letters?
787. Who can share a hundred times a day and still have a beard?
788. What plays when it works, and works when it plays?
789. What seven letters did the boy utter when he opened his piggy-bank and found nothing in it?
790. What is a boxer's favourite drink?
791. What comes with a car, is of no use to a car, and yet the car can't run without it?
792. What kind of clothing wears the longest?
793. What happens when the police take a burglar's fingerprints?
794. What animals didn't come on the ark in pairs?
795. What is the surest way to double your money?
796. What kind of person is fed up with people?

797. What is the found in the middle of both America and Australia?

798. What did the candle say to his girlfriend?

799. What is the best way to remove paint?

800. What is bacteria?

801. What is the biggest ant?

802. What was the largest island before Australia was discovered?

803. What day of the year is a command to go forward?

804. Why don't people eat gravy in China?

805. What is the poorest plant?

806. What would happen if an elephant sat in front of you at the movies?

807. What is the best way to find a pin in a rug?

808. What do well-behaved young lambs say to their mothers?

809. What do baby apes sleep in?

810. What does the Queen Mary weigh just before leaving harbour?

811. What is very light but can't be lifted?

812. What is an astronomer?

813. Why do firemen wear red braces?

814. What did one tap say to the other tap?

815. What can speak in every language but never went to school?

816. What goes up and never comes down?

817. What letter is nine inches long?

818. What is the best way to get fat?

819. What beats a good wife?

820. What two vegetables begin and end with two letters in the same order?

821. What do you lose every time you stand up?

822. What is the difference between the North Pole and the South Pole?

823. What amount of money can be divided fifty-fifty between two persons giving one person a hundred times more than the other?

824. What word of four letters still has five left when three of the letters are taken away?

825. What is oil before it is discovered?

826. What has cities with no houses, rivers without water, and forests without trees?

827. What do we all put off till tomorrow?

828. What should you say when you meet a monster, with three heads?

829. What is the difference between a retired sailor and a blind man?

830. What will stay hot in the refrigerator?

831. What branch of the army do babies join?

832. What two words have thousands of letters in them?

833. What is the difference between a dog and a flea?

834. What man always finds things dull?

835. What always ends everything?

836. What is the difference between maximum and minimum?

837. What 7-letter name has only 3 letters?

838. What was the highest mountain before Mt. Everest was discovered?

839. What is the best thing to put into a pie?

840. What code message is the same from left to right to left, upside down and right side up?

841. What is a foreign ant?

842. What is it that a man can use for shaving, cleaning his clothes and sleeping in?

843. What is the best way to keep fish from smelling?

844. What trees do fortune-tellers look at?

845. What is the difference between an organist and a cold in the head?

846. What did the fireman say when the church caught fire?

847. What word, when deprived of a letter, makes you sick?

848. What did Columbus see on his right hand when he discovered America?
849. What letters are invisible, but never out of sight?
850. What 8-letter word has one letter in it?
851. What American author may be considered equal to three-fifths of all the poets, ancient and modern?
852. What is the difference between a bright scholar and a shoe-cleaner?
853. What is the difference between a donkey and a postage stamp?
854. What is the difference between a hungry man and a greedy man?
855. What can a whole apple do that half an apple can't do?
856. What is the difference between a cat and a match?
857. What happened to the discoverer of electricity?
858. What is junk?
859. What does not move when it is fast but moves when it is not fast?
860. What is the difference between a cat and a comma?
861. What gives milk and says. 'Oom, oom'?
862. What is the difference between a beached vessel and wrecked airplane?
863. What did the boy octopus say to the girl octopus?
864. What do most gardeners not like to grow?
865. What is the difference between a thief and a church bell?
866. What is all over the house?
867. What is the shortest month?
868. What do porcupines have for dinner?
869. What is the difference between a cashier and a schoolmaster?
870. What is green and can jump a mile a minute?
871. What is it that everyone wishes for, and yet wants to get rid of as soon as it is obtained?
872. What is the difference between a beautiful girl and a mouse?

873. What did the big watch hand say to the little watch hand?
874. What dish is out of this world?
875. What is the difference between a man and a running dog?
876. What kind of clothing does a pet dog wear?
877. What is dark but made by light?
878. What happens when a flea gets very angry?
879. What would happen if you swallowed your spoon?
880. What is the latest thing in dresses?
881. What increases its value by being turned upside down?
882. What's the difference between the business of a removal firm and a shop that sells notepaper?
883. What can a man give to a woman that he can't give to a man?
884. What part of a clock is always old?
885. What do you get if you cross an elephant with a boy scout?
886. What is the difference between a china shop and a furniture shop?
887. Which country has the best appetite?
888. What kind of band doesn't make music?
889. What is the difference between a dressmaker and a farmer?
890. What is a dimple?
891. What should you always keep because nobody else wants it?
892. What can you hold without touching it?
893. What is the best thing to make in a hurry?
894. What part of London is in France?
895. What extraordinary kind of meat is to be bought in the Isle of Wight?
896. What man must have his glass before he starts to work?
897. What is free speech?
898. What 5-letter word has 6 left when you have taken 2 letters away?
899. What is a button?
900. What is the best way to hunt bear?

901. What is a piece of pie in Italian?
902. What would you call two bananas?
903. What is a doughnut?
904. What is the most disagreeable month for soldiers?
905. What happened when the little pussy swallowed a penny?
906. What part of the fish weighs the most?
907. What three letters does a wise man carry around with him?
908. What did one fish say to the other?
909. What is the difference between an old man and a cow?
910. What is the best way to win a race?
911. What happened when the man sat on a pin?
912. What time is it when a pie is equally divided among four hungry boys?
913. What does the word 'minimum' mean?
914. Where do tadpoles go to change into frogs?
915. What can you break without touching?
916. What animal makes the most of its food?
917. What did the chimney and the door do when the house caught fire?
918. What animal would you like to be on a cold day?
919. What is a paradise?
920. What time is the same spelled backward or forward?
921. What's the difference between a peeping Tom and a child just out of the bath?
922. What did the big chimney say to the little chimney?
923. What kind of bell doesn't ring?
924. What happens to people who slim?
925. What is it that occurs four times in every week, twice in every month, and only once in a year?
926. What must you keep after giving it to somebody else?
927. What happened when the dentist and manicurist fell out?
928. What dance represents two containers?
929. What has a head, a tail, four legs, and sees equally from both ends?

930. What do you call an uneducated ant?
931. What is the difference between 100 and 1000?
932. What did the old man do when he thought he was dying?
933. What happened when the wheel was invented?
934. What is most like a hen stealin'?
935. What is a good way to get wild duck?
936. What do people in America call little black cats?
937. What does a dog get when it graduates from dog school?
938. What is black, shiny, lives in trees and is very dangerous?
939. What would happen if you ate yeast and polish?
940. What is the difference between a tailor and a horse trainer?
941. What was the greatest invention in the world?
942. What two things can't you have for breakfast?
943. What is the longest sentence in the world?
944. What sick bird is unlawful?
945. What can be right but never wrong?
946. What is too much for one, enough for two, but nothing at all for three?
947. What is the best exercise for losing weight?
948. What is the difference between an ice cream cone and a bully?
949. What is it that is given to you alone, but used more by other people?
950. What did the violin say to the harp?
951. What relation is a child to its own father when it's not its own father's son?
952. What profession did the parrot decide to follow after she swallowed the clock?
953. What did the 10 pence piece say when it got stuck in the slot?
954. What happened to the fat man who sat on a flagpole to reduce?
955. What's the difference between a sunbather and someone who lives in the Sahara?
956. What can't you name without breaking it?

957. What is an easy way to make your money bigger?
958. What is a distant relative?
959. What is the difference between a bare head and a hair bed?
960. What would you call the life story of a car?
961. What do you get if you cross a chick and a guitar?
962. What is hard to beat?
963. What's the difference between an orchestral conductor and an oven?
964. What does Mexico produce that no other country produces?
965. What are the most unsociable things in the world?
966. What creature becomes healthier when beheaded?
967. What do you get if an axe hits your head?
968. What is the best way to turn people's heads?
969. What makes a road broad?
970. What does the evening wear?
971. What is a banged-up used car?
972. What always happens at the end of a dry spell?
973. What is the difference between a dog losing his hair, and a man painting a small outhouse?
974. What happened when the icicle landed on the man's head?
975. What has a name of three letters, but still has its name when two of the letters are taken away?
976. What smells most in a chemist's shop?
977. What kind of ant can count?
978. What is in fashion but always out of date?
979. What did Adam first plant in the Garden of Eden?
980. What runs along the streets in New York?
981. What person helps to bring up hundreds of people?
982. What is the hardest thing for a bald man to part with?
983. What is a sleeping bull?
984. What kind of music does a ghost like?
985. What did the dentist say to the golfer?
986. Why did the shark not bother to attack the woman in the sea.

987. What insect is religious?
988. What is better than an idea?
989. What men are most above board in their movement?
990. What nationality is Santa Claus?
991. What's the difference between a good footballer and an industrious man?
992. What is it of which the common sort is best?
993. What fish has the lowest voice?
994. What is it that someone else has to take before you can get it?
995. What kind of pine has the sharpest needles?
996. What's the difference between a music maker and a corpse?
997. What is a person called who doesn't have all his fingers on one hand?
998. What is the worst kind of fare for men to live on?
999. What animal doesn't play fair?
1000. What is drawn by everyone without pen or pencil?

Answers

751. Anchor.
752. A lighthouse.
753. A tomato in a lift.
754. It made a great hit.
755. Advice.
756. Money.
757. Rain.
758. A coffin.
759. A hole in her tights.
760. Eye.
761. 'Ours is a nice house, ours is.'
762. A ditch.
763. A safe robbery.
764. 'I'm at your service, madam.'
765. Hoe, hoe, hoe.
766. A hole.
767. Stocking.
768. Trouble.
769. Absence of body.
770. Sit on your set.
771. She gave him the cold shoulder.
772. Iced tea with lemon.
773. The police made him bring it back.
774. Tired.
775. A chop assistant.

776. Let it rain.
777. About 40 rupees.
778. 'Halo.'
779. Your breath.
780. The temperature.
781. A giraffe.
782. A T junction.
783. 'Isn't it a pity we seem to meet only when it rains?'
784. A mirror.
785. Down a road with telegraph poles, because then you can see from pole to pole.
786. Alphabet.
787. A barber.
788. A fountain.
789. O I C U R M T.
790. Punch.
791. Noise.
792. Underwear, because it is never worn out.
793. It creates a very bad impression.
794. Worms. They came in an apple.
795. Fold it—you'll find it increases.
796. A cannibal.
797. The letter R.
798. Are you going out tonight?
799. Sit down on it before it's dry.
800. The rear entrance of a cafeteria.
801. An elephant.
802. Australia.
803. March fourth.
804. Have you ever tried eating gravy with chopsticks?
805. A vine—because it can't support itself.
806. You would miss most of the picture.
807. Walk around in your bare feet.
808. 'Thank ewe!'
809. Apricots.
810. Anchor.
811. A bubble.
812. A night watchman with a college education.
813. To hold their trousers up!
814. 'You're a big drip.'
815. An echo.
816. Your age.
817. The letter Y. It is one quarter of a yard.
818. Go to the butcher's shop.
819. A bad husband.
820. Tomato and onion.
821. Your lap.
822. The whole world.
823. Fifty pounds and fifty pence.
824. Love, from this word take away L, O and E, leaving V, the Roman number five.
825. A well-kept secret.
826. A map.
827. Our clothes, when we go to bed.
828. 'Hello, hello, hello!'
829. One cannot go to sea, the other cannot see to go.

830. Mustard.
831. The infantry.
832. Post office.
833. A dog can have fleas but a flea can't have dogs.
834. A knifegrinder.
835. The letter G.
836. When a boy named Maxi won't talk, that is maximum; when a girl named Mini won't talk, that's minimum.
837. Barbara.
838. Mount Everest.
839. Your teeth.
840. S O S.
841. Important.
842. A razor, a brush and a pair of pyjamas.
843. Cut off their noses.
844. Palms.
845. One knows the stops, the other stops the nose.
846. 'Holy smoke!'
847. Music.
848. Five fingers.
849. I and S.
850. Envelope.
851. Poe.
852. One shines at the head, the other at the foot.
853. One you lick with a stick, the other you stick with a lick.
854. One longs to eat and the others eats too long.
855. It can look round.
856. One's light on its feet, the other lights on its head.

857. He got a nasty shock.
858. Something you save for years and throw away just before you need it.
859. A motorboat tied up at a dock.
860. A cat has claws at the end of its paws, a comma has a pause at the end of its clause.
861. A cow walking backwards.
862. One grounds on the land, the other lands on the ground.
863. 'I want to hold your hand, hand, hand, hand, hand,....
864. Old.
865. One steals from the people, the other peals from the steeple.
866. The roof.
867. May. It has only three letters.
868. Prickled onions.
869. One minds the till, the other tills the mind.
870. A grasshopper with hiccups.
871. A good appetite.
872. One charms the he's, the other harms the cheese.
873. 'Don't go away, I'll be back in an hour.'
874. A flying saucer.
875. One wears trousers, the other pants.
876. A petticoat.
877. A shadow.

878. It gets hopping mad.
879. You wouldn't be able to stir.
880. A nightdress.
881. The number 6.
882. One's moving, the other's stationary.
883. His name.
884. The second hand.
885. An elephant who helps old ladies across the street.
886. One sells teasets, the other sells settees.
887. Hungary.
888. A rubber band.
889. A dressmaker sews what she gathers, a farmer gathers what he sows.
890. A pimple going the other way.
891. Your temper.
892. Your breath.
893. Haste.
894. The letter N.
895. Mutton from Cowes.
896. A glazier.
897. When you can use someone else's telephone.
898. Sixty.
899. A small event that is always coming off.
900. With your clothes off.
901. A pizza pie.
902. A pair of slippers.
903. A person who is crazy about money.
904. A long March.
905. There was money in the kitty.
906. The scales.
907. A.Y.Z. (A wise head).
908. If you keep your big mouth shut, you won't get caught.
909. One lives in the past, the other in the pasture.
910. Run faster than anybody else.
911. Nothing; it was a safety pin.
912. A quarter to one.
913. A very small mother.
914. The croakroom.
915. A promise.
916. The giraffe. It makes a little go a long way.
917. The chimney flue and the door bolted.
918. A little otter.
919. Something you see in Paris.
920. Noon.
921. One is rude and nosey, the other's nude and rosy.
922. 'You are too young to smoke.'
923. A dumb-bell.
924. They have a thin time.
925. The letter E.
926. Your word.
927. They fought tooth and nail.
928. The can-can.
929. A blind mule.
930. Ignorant.
931. Naught.

932. He moved to the living room.

933. It caused a revolution.

934. A cock robin.

935. Buy a tame one and annoy it.

936. Kittens.

937. A pedigree.

938. A crow with a machine gun.

939. You would rise and shine.

940. One mends a tear, the other tends a mare.

941. The wheel because it got everything rolling.

942. Lunch and dinner.

943. 'Go to prison for life.'

944. An ill-eagle.

945. An angle.

946. A secret.

947. Pushing yourself away from the table.

948. You lick one, the other licks you.

949. Your name.

950. 'May I string along with you?'

951. Daughter.

952. Politics.

953. 'Money's tight these days.'

954. He fell off.

955. One gets tanned by the sun, the other gets sand by the ton.

956. Silence

957. Put it under a magnifying glass.

958. An uncle in Australia.

959. One fleas for shelter, the other is shelter for fleas.

960. An autobiography.

961. A chicken that makes music when you pluck it.

962. A drum with a hole in it.

963. One makes the beat. The other bakes the meat.

964. Mexicans.

965. Milestones; you never see two of them together.

966. The whale—hale.

967. A splitting headache.

968. Go to the theatre late.

969. The letter B.

970. The close of day.

971. A car in first-crash condition.

972. It rains.

973. One sheds his coat, the other coats his shed.

974. It knocked him cold.

975. Tea or Bee or Pea

976. The chemist's nose.

977. An accountant.

978. The letter F.

979. His foot.

980. The kerb.

981. The lift attendant.

982. A comb.

983. A bulldozer.

984. Haunting melodies.

985. 'You have a hole in one.'

986. It was a man-eating shark.

987. A preying mantis.

988. You, dear.

989. Chessmen.

990. North Polish.
991. One times his passes well, the other passes his time well.
992. Sense.
993. A bass.
994. Your photograph.
995. A porcupine.

996. One composes, the other decomposes.
997. Normal, fingers should be on two hands.
998. Warfare.
999. The cheetah.
1000. Breath.

1001. What kind of star wears sunglasses?

1002. What's the difference between here and there?

1003. What country makes you shiver?

1004. What is another name for a telephone kiosk?

1005. What can you hold without touching it?

1006. What did the Vikings use to keep in touch with one another?

1007. What lives on its own substance and dies when it devours itself?

1008. What's the difference between a man parking his car and a man smashing dishes?

1009. What is the best way to make trousers last?

1010. What sound do two porcupines make when they kiss?

1011. What are the little white things in your head that bite?

1012. What makes everyone sick except those who swallow it?

1013. What is a pony with a sore throat?

1014. What man makes his living only at put-up jobs?

1015. What did the surgeon say to the patient after he'd finished the operation?

1016. What did the children of Israel eat while they were in the desert?

1017. What did Robert Bruce do when he saw the spider climbing up and down?

1018. What do they call the man who winds up Big Ben?

1019. What's the difference between a pianist and sixteen ounces of lead?

1020. What is the difference between a man with no money and a feather bed?

1021. What ailment afflicts the oak tree?

1022. What happened when the electronic guitar was plugged into the lamp standard?

1023. What did the policeman say after booking a dozen motorists for illegal parking?

1024. What's the difference between a water butt and a poor cricket fielder?

1025. What did the Egyptians do when it got dark?

1026. What's the difference between the end of a queue and a letterbox?

1027. What did the kangaroo say when her baby was missing?

1028. What is a calf after it is six months old?

1029. What is a sound sleeper?

1030. What's the first thing you do in the morning?

1031. What's the difference between an ornithologist and a bad speller?

1032. What remains down even when it flies up in the air?

1033. What's the difference between a hard-hitting batman and a flea?

1034. What is the opposite of restaurant?

1035. What kind of tree do you find in the kitchen?

1036. What does C.I.D. stand for?

1037. What gets around everywhere?

1038. What's the difference between a clock and a partnership?

1039. What's the difference between a simpleton and a Welsh Rarebit?

1040. What is the difference between a boy going upstairs and a boy looking upstairs?

1041. Where did the baby ear of corn come from?

1042. What makes a tree noisy?

1043. What makes a pair of shoes?

1044. What is always before you, yet you can never see it?

1045. What is the best thing out?

1046. What has neither flesh nor bone, but has four fingers and a thumb?

1047. What did the zookeeper see when the elephant squirted water?

1048. What did the Eskimo wife say to her husband when he finished building the igloo?

1049. What happened to Lady Godiva's horse when he saw she had no clothes on?

1050. What professional man works with a will?

1051. What did the sardine call the submarine?

1052. What is the only kind of pain of which one makes light?

1053. What salad do lovers prefer?

1054. What has a big mouth but can't talk?

1055. What kind of dog would believe you to ask you the time?

1056. What kind of animal has red spots?

1057. What kind of kitten works for the St. John's Ambulance Brigade?

1058. What is the difference between a gardener and a billiard player?

1059. What paper should make the best kites?

1060. What instruments do you carry in your ears?

1061. What did the coward say to the stamp?

1062. What's the difference between a whale-hunter and a happy dog?

1063. What do you do to stop your nose from running?

1064. What is the difference between a blacksmith and a safe mare?

1065. What fish might you find in a bird cage?

1066. Why is an acrobat an agreeable person to know?

1067. What happened to the frog when it died?

1068. What is a lawyer's favourite pudding?

1069. What should you do if you see two snails fighting?

1070. What is the most suitable dance to wind up a frolic?

1071. What did the ram say to his girlfriend?

1072. What miracles happened when Mr. Stone and Mr. Wood watched a pretty girl pass by?

1073. What horses keep late hours?

1074. What is the difference between a man with an unnatural voice and one with unnatural teeth?

1075. What is the difference between a crazy rabbit and a counterfeit coin?

1076. What animals are poor dancers?

1077. What is as round as the moon, as black as coal, and has a hole in the middle?

1078. What happened when the dwarf applied for a job in the circus?

1079. What is the difference between a pen and a pencil?

1080. What trade is it in which no man will get on unless he sticks to it?

1081. What has a head but no brain?

1082. What is the difference between a milkmaid on the farm and a seagull?

1083. What is it that is alive and has only one foot?

1084. Who was the fastest runner in history?

1085. What do historians talk about when they meet?

1086. What words can be pronounced quicker and shorter by adding another syllable to them?

1087. What is as big as an elephant but doesn't weigh anything?

1088. What is it that you can take away the whole and still have some left?

1089. What is the difference between a volcano and a butterfly?

1090. What did the porcupine say to the cactus?

1091. What person always falls down on the job?

1092. What is the difference between the earth and the sea?

1093. What musical key cannot vote?

1094. What is it that you cannot hold for ten minutes, though it is lighter than a feather?

1095. What asks no questions but gets a great many answers?

1096. What is the difference between a book and a bore?

1097. What artist puts money away for a rainy day?

1098. What is a prickly pear?

1099. What is the difference between a king's son, a monkey's mother, a bald head and an orphan?

1100. What's the difference between Noah's Ark and Joan of Arc?

1101. What has four legs like an elephant, a trunk like an elephant, looks just like an elephant, but is not an elephant?

1102. What is the difference between a banana and a bell?

1103. What did the patient say to the anesthetist?

1104. What's the difference between a jigsaw expert and a greedy boy?

1105. What does a lamppost become when the lamp is removed?

1106. What ship is always managed by more than one person?

1107. What is the difference between a greedy person and an electric toaster?

1108. What is a bulldozer?

1109. What's a bikini?

1110. What are the best kind of stockings for cricketers to wear?

1111. What is more to be admired than a promising young man?

1112. What person tries to make you smile most of the time?

1113. What is worse than biting into an apple and finding a worm?

1114. What is the hardest key to turn?

1115. What is the best thing to take when you are run down?

1116. What nail does a carpenter not like to hit?

1117. What is neither inside a house nor outside a house, but no house would be complete without it?

1118. What overpowers you without hurting you?

1119. What kind of tea makes you feel brave?

1120. What letter should you avoid?

1121. What did the city commuter miss most living out in the country?

1122. What kind of doctor treats ducks?

1123. What is worse than being with a fool?

1124. What always comes into a house through the keyhole?

1125. What are government workers called in Seville?
1126. What bird can lift the most?
1127. What does a caterpillar do on New Year's day?
1128. What do liars do after they die?
1129. What did the rabbit want to do when it grew up?
1130. What do you call a fast duck?
1131. What did the skunk say when the wind suddenly changed direction?
1132. What kind of geese are found in Portugal?
1133. What do Chinese lumberjacks use to fell trees?
1134. What famous detective liked to take bubble baths?
1135. What does an envelope say when you lick it?
1136. What is a Mexican weather report?
1137. What kind of bath can you take without water?
1138. What do you get if you cross an insect and a rabbit?
1139. What did the bee say to the flower?
1140. What did the tree say to the flypaper?
1141. What ten letter word starts with g-a-s?
1142. What kind of apple has a short temper?
1143. What kind of watch is best for people who don't like time on their hands?
1144. What goes up and down but doesn't move?
1145. What word, if pronounced right, is wrong but if pronounced wrong is right?
1146. What has four legs and a back but no body?
1147. What did the man do when he got a big gas bill?
1148. What is the best day to go to the beach?
1149. What kind of bulbs don't need water?
1150. What trees come in two's?
1151. What animal doesn't believe anything?
1152. What is the first thing you see when you understand something?
1153. What people travel the most?
1154. What person is always in a hurry?

1155. What people are like the end of a book?
1156. What flowers does everyone have?
1157. What did the light switch say to the girl?
1158. What kind of coach has no wheels?
1159. What is the first thing you put into a room?
1160. What did one arithmetic book say to the other arithmetic book?
1161. What has two hands but no arms?
1162. What piece of wood is like a king?
1163. What do people make that you can't see?
1164. What did the boy squirrel say to the girl squirrel?
1165. What did the girl squirrel answer back?
1166. What kind of table has no legs?
1167. What cap is never removed?
1168. What did one car muffler say to the other car muffler?
1169. What did the father tree say to his son?
1170. What has teeth but no mouth?
1171. What kind of money do monsters use?
1172. What is a parrot?
1173. What knights rode camels?
1174. What is a sleeping bag?
1175. What is the most valuable fish?
1176. What is a ghost's favourite rock?
1177. What do you call a greasy chicken?
1178. What is the difference between a tickle and a wise guy?
1179. What did Napoleon become after his 39th year?
1180. What is a wet cat?
1181. What do you get if you cross a cat with a laughing hyena?
1182. What kind of lock is on a hippie's door?
1183. What is a very hard subject?
1184. What kind of key opens a casket?
1185. What is a broken down hot rod?
1186. What is ice?
1187. What sea creature can add?

1188. What have eyes but can't see?

1189. What did the girl watch say to the boy watch?

1190. What is the science of shopping?

1191. What is a good way to get fat?

1192. What food is good for the brain?

1193. What did Tennessee?

1194. What has fifty heads and fifty tails?

1195. What kind of bird is like a letter?

1196. What do you draw without a pencil or paper?

1197. What is the left side of an apple?

1198. What are southern fathers called?

1199. What goes around in circles and makes kids happy?

1200. What kind of cattle laugh?

1201. What is a bee with a low buzz?

1202. What pet is always found on the floor?

1203. What is the proverb about catching a cold?

1204. What happened to the wolf who fell into the washing machine?

1205. What did the boy firefly say to the girl firefly?

1206. What musical instrument from Spain helps you fish?

1207. What is the difference between a fish and a piano?

1208. What has four wheels and flies?

1209. What do you call a boy named Lee whom no one wants to talk to?

1210. What did one tooth say to the other tooth?

1211. What is the first thing ghosts do when they get into cars?

1212. What do you call your mother's other sister?

1213. What tree is hairy?

1214. What musical instrument doesn't tell the truth?

1215. What part of a car is the laziest?

1216. What is a panther?

1217. What did the pen say to the paper?

1218. What does a duck wear when he gets married?

1219. What fruit would a gorilla like to sleep on?

1220. What did the beaver say to the tree?
1221. What did the buffalo say to his son when he went away on a long trip?
1222. What is an ant dictator?
1223. What is a bee?
1224. What do you call a bee born in May?
1225. What colour was the "Keep off the Grass" sign?
1226. What letter stands for a drink?
1227. What geometric figure is like a runaway parrot?
1228. What animal is a cannibal?
1229. What did the werewolf write on his Christmas cards?
1230. What did one raindrop say to the other raindrop?
1231. What did the bookworm say to the librarian?
1232. What do ants use for hula hoops?
1233. What means of transportation gives people colds?
1234. What would you call a small wound?
1235. What kind of television programme tells you who just broke an arm or leg?
1236. What is the difference between a hill and a pill?
1237. What is the famous last word in surgery?
1238. What sickness do cowboys get from riding wild horses?
1239. What is a sick crocodile?
1240. What is the difference between a boxer and a man with a cold?
1241. What do cowboys call a doctor's hypodermic needle?
1242. What do you get if you put your head in a washing machine?
1243. What did the doctor say to the tonsil?
1244. What has fifty legs but can't walk?
1245. What is worse than a centipede with a sore feet?
1246. What is worse than a giraffe with a sore throat?
1247. What is worse than a turtle with claustrophobia?
1248. What do seven days of dieting do?

1249. What do you have if your head is hot, your feet are cold and you see spots in front of your eyes?

1250. What did Frankenstein say when a bolt of lightning hit him?

Answers

1001. A film star.
1002. The letter T.
1003. Chile.
1004. A chatterbox.
1005. A conversation.
1006. The Norse Code.
1007. A candle.
1008. One sets the brakes, the other breaks the sets.
1009. Make the coat and waistcoat first.
1010. 'Ouch!'
1011. Teeth.
1012. Flattery.
1013. A little hoarse.
1014. A paper-hanger.
1015. 'That's enough out of you.'
1016. The sand which is there.
1017. He went and invented the yo-yo.
1018. A big time operator.
1019. One pounds away, the other weighs a pound.
1020. One is hard up, the other is soft down.
1021. A corn.
1022. It played light music.
1023. 'I've dona fine day's work.'
1024. One catches the drops, the other drops the catches.
1025. They turned on the Israelites.
1026. One makes the tail, the other takes the mail.
1027. 'My pockets' been picked!'
1028. Seven months old.
1029. Someone who snores.
1030. You wake up.
1031. One's a bird watcher, the other's a word botcher.
1032. A feather.
1033. One's a ball smiter, the other's a small biter.
1034. Workerant.
1035. A pantry.
1036. Copper in disguise.
1037. Belts.
1038. When a clock is wound up it goes; when a partnership is wound up, it stops.
1039. One's easy to cheat, the other's cheesy to eat.
1040. One is stepping up the stairs, the other is staring up the steps.
1041. The stalk brought it.
1042. Its bark.
1043. Two shoes.
1044. Your future.
1045. An aching tooth.
1046. A glove.

1047. A jumbo jet.
1048. What an ice house!
1049. It made him shy.
1050. A solicitor.
1051. A can with people in it.
1052. A window-pane.
1053. Lettuce alone.
1054. A jar.
1055. A watchdog.
1056. A leopard with measles.
1057. A first-aid kit.
1058. One minds his peas, the other minds his cues.
1059. Fly paper.
1060. Drums.
1061. 'I can lick you.'
1062. One tags his whale, the other wags his tail.
1063. Put your foot out and trip it up.
1064. One is horse shoer, the other is a sure horse.
1065. A perch.
1066. He is always doing a good turn.
1067. It just croaked.
1068. Sue-it.
1069. Leave them alone and let them slug it out.
1070. A reel.
1071. 'I love ewe!'
1072. Stone turned to wood and wood turned to stone. They both turned to look, and the girl turned into a restaurant.
1073. Nightmares.
1074. One has a false set to voice, the other false set o'teeth.
1075. One is a mad bunny, the other is bad money.
1076. Four-legged ones, because they have two left feet.
1077. A gramophone record.
1078. He was put on the short list.
1079. You push a pen, but a pencil has to be lead.
1080. Bill-posting.
1081. A cabbage.
1082. One skims milk, the other skims water.
1083. A leg.
1084. Adam—he was the first in the human race.
1085. Old times.
1086. 'Quick' and 'short'.
1087. An elephant's shadow.
1088. The word 'wholesome'.
1089. In one the lava comes out of the crater, in the other the cater (pillar) comes out of the larva.
1090. Are you my mother?'
1091. A paratrooper.
1092. One is dirty, the other is tide-y.
1093. A minor.
1094. Your breath.
1095. A doorbell.
1096. You can shut up a book.
1097. A pavement artist.
1098. Two porcupines.

1099. The king's son is the heir apparent, a monkey's mother is a hairy parent, a bald head has no hair apparent, and an orphan has nary a parent.

1100. One was made of wood, the other was Maid of Orleans.

1101. A picture of a elephant.

1102. You can peel the banana only once.

1103. 'Because of you I've been considerably put out.'

1104. One's is a good puzzler, the other's a pud guzzler.

1105. A lamplighter.

1106. Partnership.

1107. One takes the most and the other makes the toast.

1108. Someóne who sleeps while a politician is making a speech.

1109. A space suit.

1110. Stockings with runs in them.

1111. A paying one.

1112. A photographer.

1113. Finding half a worm.

1114. A donkey.

1115. The number of the car that hit you.

1116. His fingernail.

1117. A window.

1118. Sleep.

1119. Safety.

1120. The letter A because it makes men mean.

1121. The last train home at night.

1122. A quack.

1123. Fooling with a bee.

1124. A key.

1125. Seville servants.

1126. A crane.

1127. Turns over a new leaf.

1128. Lie still.

1129. He wanted to join the hare force.

1130. A quick quack.

1131. "It all comes back to me now".

1132. Portu-geese.

1133. Chopsticks (what else?).

1134. Sherlock Foams.

1135. Nothing. It just shuts up.

1136. Chili today, hot tamale.

1137. A sun bath.

1138. Bugs Bunny.

1139. "Hello, honey!"

1140. "I'm stuck on you."

1141. Automobile.

1142. A crab apple.

1143. A pocket watch.

1144. A staircase.

1145. Wrong.

1146. A chair.

1147. He exploded.

1148. Sunday.

1149. Light bulbs.

1150. Pear (pair) trees.

1151. Sheep. They always say, "Bah! Bah!"

1152. You see the light.

1153. Romans.

1154. A Russian.
1155. The Finnish.
1156. Tulips (two lips).
1157. "You turn me on."
1158. A football coach.
1159. Your feet.
1160. "Boy, do I have problems!"
1161. A clock.
1162. A ruler.
1163. Noise.
1164. "I'm nuts about you."
1165. "You're nuts, so bad yourself."
1166. A multiplication table.
1167. Your kneecap.
1168. "Am I exhausted!"
1169. "You're a chip off the old block."
1170. A comb or a saw.
1171. Weirdo (weired dough).
1172. A wordy birdy.
1173. The Arabian Nights (knights).
1174. A knapsack (nap sack).
1175. Goldfish.
1176. Tombstone.
1177. A slick chick.
1178. One is fun, the other thinks he's fun.
1179. 40 years old.
1180. A drizzle puss.
1181. A giggle puss.
1182. A padlock.
1183. The study of rocks.
1184. A skeleton key.
1185. A shot rod.
1186. Skid stuff.
1187. An octoplus.
1188. Needles, storms and potatoes.
1189. "Keep your hands to yourself."
1190. Biology (buy-ology).
1191. Fry up some bacon.
1192. Noodle soup.
1193. He saw what Arkansas.
1194. Fifty pennies.
1195. A jaybird.
1196. A window shade.
1197. The part that you don't eat.
1198. Southpaws.
1199. A merry-go-round.
1200. Laughing stock.
1201. A mumble bee.
1202. A carpet.
1203. "Win a flu (few), lose a flu."
1204. He became a wash and werewolf.
1205. "I glow for you."
1206. A cast-a-net (castanet).
1207. You can't tuna a fish.
1208. A garbage truck.
1209. Lonely (Lone-Lee).
1210. "There's gold in them that fills."
1211. They fasten their sheet (seat) belts.
1212. Deodorant (the other aunt).
1213. A poplar (popular) tree.
1214. A lyre (liar).
1215. The wheels. They are always tired.

1216. Someone who makes panths (pants).
1217. "I dot an 'i' on you."
1218. A duxedo (tuxedo).
1219. An ape-ri-cot (apricot).
1220. "It's been nice gnawing (knowing) you."
1221. "Bison!" ("Bye, son!")
1222. A tyrant.
1223. An insect that stings (sings) for its supper.
1224. A maybe.
1225. G'way (gray).
1226. The letter T.
1227. A polygon (Polly gone).
1228. An anteater (aunt eater).
1229. "Best vicious (wishes) of the season."
1230. "My plop is bigger than your plop."
1231. "Can I burrow (borrow) this book?"
1232. Cheerios.
1233. A choo-choo train.
1234. A short cut.
1235. A newscast.

1236. A hill is hard to get up, a pill is hard to get down.
1237. "Ouch!"
1238. Bronchitis (bronc-itis).
1239. An illigator.
1240. A boxer knows his blows, a man with a cold blows his nose.
1241. A sick (six) shooter.
1242. Cleaner and brighter thoughts.
1243. "You look so cute, I think I'll take you out."
1244. Half a centipede.
1245. A giraffe with a sore throat.
1246. A turtle with claustrophobia.
1247. An elephant with hay fever.
1248. They make one weak (week).
1249. You probably have a polka-dotted sock over your head.
1250. "Thanks, I needed that!"

1251. What did the doctor find when he examined the X-ray of the dummy's head?

1252. What goes, "Ho, ho, ho, plop!"?

1253. What happened when a dog swallowed the watch?

1254. What is a drill sergeant?

1255. What would happen if you swallowed uranium?

1256. What is the heathiest kind of water?

1257. What is the perfect cure for dandruff?

1258. What did the nervous kid say when the doctor asked if he had been getting enough iron?

1259. What does every drowning person say no matter what language he speaks?

1260. What do you get if you put your hand in a pot?

1261. What did the woman say when the doctor asked if she smoked cigarettes?

1262. What is the best way to cure acid indigestion?

1263. What is the difference between a person asleep and a person awake?

1264. What happened when the horse swallowed a dollar bill?

1265. What game do you play if you don't take care of your teeth?

1266. What kind of gun does a bee shoot?

1267. What do witches eat?

1268. What criminal doesn't take baths?

1269. What dog is religious?

1270. What is yellow and wears a mask?

1271. What did the mother elephant say to the baby elephant when it misbehaved?

1272. What kind of long-distance calls do ministers make when they speak to each other?

1273. What did the banana do when the monkey chased it?

1274. What is a crazy pickle?

1275. What kind of cake should you serve to chicken?

1276. What did the eggs say when it was put in the pot?

1277. What hired killer never goes to jail?

1278. What is small, purple and dangerous?

1279. What do you get when two strawberries meet?

1280. What is a hippie mummy?

1281. What did the father mummy say to the kid mummy when he asked for candy?

1282. What cruel person would sit on a baby?

1283. What gun does a police dog use?

1284. What is a policeman's favourite snack?

1285. What happens when a ghost is set on fire?

1286. What is a ghost's favourite drink in hot weather?

1287. What did the girl spirit say to the boy spirit?

1288. What kind of food do brave soldiers eat?

1289. What is stolen candy?

1290. What did the mother ghost say to the child ghost?

1291. What is the thing you eat before you die?

1292. What did the burglar give his wife for her birthday?

1293. What did the apple say to the apple pie?

1294. What is a jittery sorceress?

1295. What dog has bad manners?

1296. What kind of bird do crooks hate?

1297. What is Count Dracula's favourite snack?

1298. What is Dracula's favourite ice cream dish?

1299. What kind of cookie must be handled carefully?

1300. What kind of person loves cocoa?

1301. What kind of monster is never around when you need him?

1302. What did the mother ghost tell the kid ghost when he went out to play?

1303. What happens to naughty pigs?

1304. What do you call nervous insects?

1305. What do people do in China when it rains?

1306. What is the snappiest snake?

1307. What do you get if you cross a worm and a fur coat?

1308. What do you get if you cross a kangaroo and raccoon?

1309. What do you get if you cross a skunk and a bee?

1310. What insect is like the top of a house?

1311. What is the difference between a train and a teacher?

1312. What do flies say when it rains?

1313. What is a hot and noisy duck?

1314. What kind of horse comes from Pennsylvania?

1315. What do you always leave behind because they are dirty?

1316. What is the best way to raise strawberries?

1317. What did one shrub say to the other shrub?

1318. What did the tree say to the axe?

1319. What did the cotton plant say to the farmer?

1320. What is a ticklish subject?

1321. What is the dirtiest word in the world?

1322. What helps keep your teeth together?

1323. What do Indians raise that you can get lost in?

1324. What kind of fish performs operations?

1325. What bunch of animals can always be heard?

1326. What do you call cattle that sit on the grass?

1327. What is the brightest fish?

1328. What brings the monster's babies?

1329. What are arithmetic bugs?

1330. What animal talks a lot?

1331. What animal talks the most?

1332. What goes snap, crackle, pop?

1333. What did the father firefly say to his son?

1334. What did one firefly say to the other firefly when his light went out?

1335. What happens to grapes that worry too much?

1336. What did Ben Franklin say when he discovered that lightning was electricity?

1337. What is the difference between lightning and electricity?

1338. What children live in the ocean?

1339. What insect curses in a low voice?

1340. What insects talk too much?

1341. What did the mother worm say to the little worm who was late?

1342. What did one termite say to the other termite when he saw a house burning?

1343. What did the grasshopper say to the cockroach?

1344. What did one toad say to the other toad?

1345. What did the coughing frog say to the other frog?

1346. What sea creature has to have a good reason for doing anything?

1347. What is the correct thing to do before the King of Trees?

1348. What is the biggest building?

1349. What is the best way to catch an elephant?

1350. What is the biggest fly swatter?

1351. What is the best way to hold a bat?

1352. What is a midget skunk called?

1353. What is the distance between a stupid person's ears?

1354. What is a very small frankfurter?

1355. What is a small laugh in Indian language?

1356. What dog is 100 years old?

1357. What is the longest shortest word?

1358. What is the craziest tree?

1359. What flower is happiest?

1360. What is the hottest day of the week?

1361. What is the hottest part of a man's face?

1362. What side of a fire is the hottest?

1363. What person adds best in hot weather?
1364. What is the laziest mountain on the world?
1365. What are the laziest animals on the farm?
1366. What is the most tired vegetable?
1367. What birds are noisiest?
1368. What person has the loudest voice?
1369. What is the smartest animal?
1370. What animal grows the fastest?
1371. What is the strongest animal?
1372. What is the important subject a witch learns in witch school?
1373. What is the biggest baseball team?
1374. What is the quietest sport?
1375. What is the easiest way to make a banana split?
1376. What disease makes you better in sports?
1377. What coat has the most sleeves?
1378. What is the easiest way to grow tall?
1379. What is more invisible than an invisible man?
1380. What is the best way to catch a squirrel?
1381. What is the best key to have?
1382. What fruit has been known since man invented the calendar?
1383. What cake is as hard as a rock?
1384. What food do monster children hate most?
1385. What do you call a high-priced barber shop?
1386. What is green, has two legs and a trunk?
1387. What do you call an Indian woman who complains a lot?
1388. What kind of ears do trains have?
1389. What is a drill team?
1390. What is an astronaut's favourite meal?
1391. What can you serve but never eat?
1392. What is the difference between an umbrella and a person who never stops talking?
1393. What is a wisecrack?

1394. What is lemonade?

1395. What socks do you find in your back yard?

1396. What kind of test does a vampire take at school?

1397. What is the best way to prevent milk from turning sour?

1398. What is blue, green, yellow, purple, brown, black and grey?

1399. What do you do with dogs when you go shopping?

1400. What is a dog catcher?

1401. What did the two vampires do from midnight to 12:10?

1402. What happened when the man asked the salesman for a good belt?

1403. What did one skunk say to the other?

1404. What did one pig say to the other pig?

1405. What did the fly say when he landed on the book?

1406. What is 10+5 minus 15? What is 3+6 minus 9? What is 17+3 minus 20?

1407. What is the difference between twice twenty-two and twice two and twenty?

1408. What is the best way to cure someone who walks in his sleep?

1409. What kind of car do werewolves buy?

1410. What would you call a grandfather clock?

1411. What is a stupid flower?

1412. What can you do with old bowling balls?

1413. What room can you bounce around in?

1414. What fish do pelicans eat?

1415. What would happen if you swallowed a frog?

1416. What is the best way to get rid of flies?

1417. What is a grasshopper?

1418. What did one mountain say to the other mountain after an earthquake?

1419. What did the little light bulb say to its mother?

1420. What kind of transport do wizards like best?

1421. What makes more noise than a squealing pig?

1422. What happened when Abel died?

1423. What happens to a refrigerator when you pull its plug?
1424. What is a tongue twister?
1425. What does an invisible baby drink?
1426. What is a briefcase?
1427. What did King Kong say when he saw the Statue of Liberty?
1428. What did the invisible man call his mum and dad?
1429. What lottery did the broom win?
1430. What keys won't open doors?
1431. What goes out black and comes in white?
1432. What kind of tickle doesn't make you laugh?
1433. What kind of pool can't you swim in?
1434. What goes through a door but never goes in or out?
1435. What magazine do gardeners read?
1436. What baby is born with whiskers?
1437. What kind of coat has no sleeves, no buttons, no pockets and won't keep you warm?
1438. What lives in winter, dies in summer, and grows with its roots upwards?
1439. What is the hardest thing about learning to skate?
1440. What is locomotion?
1441. What is plowed but never planted?
1442. What is a dark horse?
1443. What is on your arm and in the sea?
1444. What animals follow everywhere you go?
1445. What do elephants have that no other animals have?
1446. What is shaped like a box, has no feet and runs up and down?
1447. What is an Eskimo father?
1448. What will happen if you talk when there is food in your mouth?
1449. What does grass say when it is cut?
1450. What colour is rain?
1451. What goes through water but doesn't get wet?

1452. What is a small cad?

1453. What can you put in a glass but never take out of it?

1454. What goes from side to side, and up and down, but never moves?

1455. What pointed in one direction and headed in the other?

1456. What is in the middle of March?

1457. What kind of car drives over water?

1458. What is the difference between a truthful person and a liar?

1459. What is the centre of gravity?

1460. What kind of beans won't grow in a garden?

1461. What is the difference between a racer and a locomotive engineer?

1462. What newspaper did the caveman read?

1463. What holiday does Dracula celebrate in November?

1464. What is a perfect name for a selfish girl?

1465. What is a musical pickle?

1466. What kind of inning does a monster baseball game have?

1467. What is the favourite ride of ghost children?

1468. What amusement park ride breaks up romances?

1469. What kind of musician can't you trust?

1470. What kind of book does Frankenstein like to read?

1471. When were there only three vowels in the alphabet?

1472. When are circus acrobats needed in restaurants?

1473. When can a man be 6 feet tall and short at the same time?

1474. When are eyes not eyes?

1475. When is a sailor not a sailor?

1476. When does a boat show affection?

1477. When does a wooden floor feel cold?

1478. When is a schoolboy like a postage stamp?

1479. When they take out an appendix, it's an appendectomy; when they remove your tonsils, it's a tonsillectomy. What is it when they remove a growth from your head?

1480. When is a woman deformed?

1481. When is a black dog not a black dog?
1482. When you look around on a cold winter's day, what do you see on every hand?
1483. When is a chair like a woman's dress?
1484. When is the only time a man is really immersed in his business?
1485. When does an MP feel girlish?
1486. When does a timid girl turn to stone?
1487. When is a newspaper like a delicate child?
1488. When should a pub landlord go to an iron foundry?
1489. When can't astronauts land on the moon?
1490. When did the fly fly?
1491. When is an apple not an apple?
1492. When is it bad luck to have a black cat following you?
1493. When is a man two men?
1494. When do crooks wear braces?
1495. When is a cow not a cow?
1496. When is man like a dog?
1497. When can you jump over three men without getting up?
1498. When the circus giant asked the dwarf to lend him a pound note, what did the dwarf say?
1499. When is a captain of a ship in love?
1500. When was the boy twins?

Answers

1251. Nothing.
1252. Santa Claus laughing his head off.
1253. He got a lot of ticks.
1254. An army dentist.
1255. You would get automic ache (a stomach ache).
1256. Well water.
1257. Baldness.
1258. "Yes, I chew my nails every day."
1259. "Glub, glub!"
1260. A potted palm.
1261. "Of cough"!
1262. Stop drinking acid.
1263. With some people it's hard to tell the difference.
1264. He bucked.

1265. Tooth (truth) or consequences.
1266. A bee-bee gun.
1267. Halloweenies (hollow wienies).
1268. A dirty crook.
1269. A praying dog.
1270. The Lone Lemon.
1271. "Tusk, tusk!"
1272. Parson-to-parson (person-to-person).
1273. The banana split.
1274. A daffydill.
1275. Layer cake.
1276. "Boy, am I in hot water!"
1277. The exterminator.
1278. A grape with a machine gun.
1279. A strawberry shake.
1280. A deady-o.
1281. "You just had some a century ago!"
1282. A baby sitter.
1283. A dogmatic.
1284. Copcakes (cupcakes).
1285. You get roast ghost.
1286. Ice-ghoul (cool) lemonade.
1287. "You don't stand a ghost of a chance with me."
1288. Her sandwiches.
1289. Hot chocolate.
1290. "Don't spook until you're spooken to."
1291. You bite the dust.
1292. A stole.
1293. "You've got some crust."
1294. A twitch.
1295. A pointer—pointing is not polite.
1296. A stool pigeon.
1297. A fangfurter (frankfurter).
1298. A blood sundae.
1299. Ginger snaps.
1300. A coconut.
1301. A werewolf because you always say, "Werewolf (where wolf)?"
1302. "Don't get your sheets dirty!"
1303. They become divided ham.
1304. Jitterbugs.
1305. Let it rain.
1306. A garter snake.
1307. A caterpillar.
1308. A fur coat with pockets.
1309. An animal that stinks as it stings.
1310. A tick (attic).
1311. A train goes "Choo-choo," but a teacher tells you to take the gum out of your mouth.
1312. "If this keeps up, my name will be mud."
1313. A firequacker.
1314. A filly (Philly).
1315. Your footprints.
1316. With a spoon.
1317. "Am I bushed!"
1318. "I'm stumped."
1319. "Stop picking on me!"
1320. The study of feathers.
1321. Pollution.

1322. Toothpaste.

1323. Maize (maze).

1324. A sturgeon (surgeon).

1325. Cattle, because they go around in herds.

1326. Ground beef.

1327. Sunfish.

1328. Frankenstork.

1329. Mosquitoes. They add to misery, subtract from pleasure, divide your attention, and multiply quickly.

1330. A yak.

1331. A yackety-yak.

1332. A firefly with a short circuit.

1333. "For a little fellow you're very bright."

1334. "Give me a push. My battery is dead."

1335. They get wrinkled and turn into raisins.

1336. Nothing. He was too shocked.

1337. We pay for electricity.

1338. Life buoys (boys).

1339. A locust.

1340. Moths. They are always chewing the rag.

1341. "Where in the earth have you been?"

1342. "Barbecue tonight!"

1343. "Bug, you man me!"

1344. "One more game of leapfrog and I'll croak."

1345. "I must have a person in my throat."

1346. A porpoise (purpose).

1347. Bough (bow).

1348. The library. It has the most stories.

1349. Act like a nut and he'll follow you anywhere.

1350. A baseball bat.

1351. By the wings.

1352. A shrunk skunk.

1353. Next to nothing.

1354. An itsy bitsy, teeny wienie.

1355. A Minnehaha.

1356. A sentry (century) dog.

1357. Abbreviation.

1358. A knotty (nutty) pine.

1359. Gladiolus.

1360. Friday (Fry day).

1361. His sideburns.

1362. The fireside.

1363. A summer.

1364. Mt. Everest.

1365. Chickens. They are always laying (lying) around.

1366. A beet (beat).

1367. Whooping cranes.

1368. The ice-cream (I scream) man.

1369. A skunk, because it makes a lot of scents (sense).

1370. A kangaroo. It grows by leaps and bounds.

1371. The snail because he is always pinching pennies.

1372. Spelling.

1373. The Giants.

1374. Bowling, because you can hear a pin drop.

1375. Cut it in half.

1376. Athlete's foot.

1377. A coat of arms.

1378. Sleep long.

1379. The shadow of an invisible man.

1380. Climb up a tree and act like a nut.

1381. Lucky.

1382. Dates.

1383. Marble cake.

1384. Cremated (creamed) spinach.

1385. A clip joint.

1386. A seasick tourist.

1387. A squaw-ker.

1388. Engineers (engine ears).

1389. A group of dentists who work together.

1390. Launch.

1391. A tennis ball.

1392. The umbrella can be shut up.

1393. An educated hole in the wall.

1394. When you help an old lemon cross the street.

1395. Garden hose.

1396. A blood test.

1397. Leave it in the cow.

1398. A box of crayons.

1399. Leave them in the barking (parking) lot.

1400. A Spot remover.

1401. They took a coffin (coffee) break.

1402. "O.K., you asked for it," the salesman said as he gave him a good belt.

1403. "So do you!"

1404. "Let's be pen pals."

1405. "I think I've read this story before."

1406. All that work for nothing!

1407. One is 44, the other is 24.

1408. Put tacks on the floor.

1409. A Wolfwagen.

1410. An old timer.

1411. A blooming idiot.

1412. Give them to elephants to shoot marbles.

1413. A ballroom.

1414. Anything that fits the bill.

1415. You might croak.

1416. Sign up some good outfielders.

1417. An insect on a pogo stick.

1418. "It's not my fault."

1419. "I love you watts and watts."

1420. Witchcraft.

1421. Two squealing pigs.

1422. He became unable.

1423. It loses its cool.

1424. When your tang gets all tongueled up.

1425. Evaporated milk.

1426. A short lawsuit.

1427. "Are you my mother?"

1428. Transparents.

1429. The sweepstakes.

1430. Don-keys, mon-keys, tur-keys.

1431. A black cow in a snowstorm.

1432. A tickle in your throat.

1433. A car pool.
1434. A keyhole.
1435. The Weeder's Digest.
1436. A kitten.
1437. A coat of paint.
1438. An icicle.
1439. The ice.
1440. A crazy dance.
1441. Snow.
1442. A nightmare.
1443. A muscle (mussel).
1444. Your calves.
1445. Baby elephants.
1446. An elevator.
1447. A cold pop.
1448. You will have said a mouthful.
1449. "I don't mow (know)."
1450. Water colour.
1451. A ray of light.
1452. A caddy.
1453. A crack.
1454. A road.
1455. A pin.
1456. The letter R.
1457. Any kind of car, if it goes over a bridge.
1458. One lies when he sleeps, the other lies all the time.
1459. The letter V.
1460. Jelly beans.
1461. One is trained to run, the other runs a train.
1462. The Prehistoric Times.
1463. Fangsgiving (Thanksgiving).
1464. Mimi (me, me).
1465. A piccolo.
1466. Frightening (fright inning).
1467. The roller ghoster (coaster).
1468. A merry-go-round. When the ride is over, people stop going around with each other.
1469. Someone who plays the bull fiddle.
1470. A novel with a cemetery plot.
1471. Before U and I were born.
1472. When tumblers are required on the tables.
1473. When he's short of money.
1474. When the wind makes them water.
1475. When he's aloft.
1476. When it hugs the shore.
1477. When it is parquet (Parky).
1478. When he is licked and put in a corner.
1479. A haircut.
1480. When mending socks, because she then has hands where her feet should be.
1481. When it's a greyhound.
1482. A glove.
1483. When it is sat in.
1484. When he is giving a swimming lesson.
1485. When he makes his maiden speech.
1486. When she becomes a little bolder.
1487. When it is weekly.

1488. When he wants a barmaid.
1489. When it is full.
1490. When the spider spied her.
1491. When it's a pineapple.
1492. When you are a mouse.
1493. When he's beside himself.
1494. When they are hold-up men.

1495. When she is turned into pasture.
1496. When he's a boxer.
1497. In a game of draughts.
1498. 'I'm sorry, but I'm terribly short.'
1499. When he seeks a mate.
1500. In a picture taken when he was two.

1501. When do you get that run-down feeling?

1502. When you go to bed why are your shoes like deferred tasks?

1503. When is it easiest to see through a man?

1504. When does water resemble a gymnast?

1505. When is a horse like a bad egg?

1506. When a lemon calls for assistance, what does it want?

1507. When will a net hold water?

1508. When is your mind like a rumpled bed?

1509. When will water stop running downhill?

1510. When is longhand quicker than shorthand?

1511. When is a new baby not the usual delicate pink?

1512. When is it correct to say, 'I is?'

1513. When a boy falls into water, what is the first thing he does?

1514. When are people smartest?

1515. When is a car not a car?

1516. When is a poor church collection like a policeman's helmet?

1517. What did one loom say to the other?

1518. What is the best cure for water on the knee?

1519. When Adam introduced himself to Eve, what three words did he use which read the same backward and forwards?

1520. When do clocks die?

1521. When a shoemaker makes a shoe, what's the first thing he uses?

1522. When do 2 and 2 make more than 2?

1523. When is a window like a star?

1524. When would you be glad to be down and out?

1525. When is a door not a door?

1526. When should you feed tiger's milk to a baby?

1527. When is a nail like a horse?

1528. When does a caterpillar grow good?

1529. When is rock not a rock?

1530. Why do elephants have ivory tusks?

1531. When is the best time to go to bed?

1532. When is a school kid like a rope?

1533. When a dirty kid has finished taking a bath, what is still dirty?

1534. When does a chair dislike you?

1535. When is the moon heaviest?

1536. When is it difficult to get your watch off your wrist?

1537. When is a grown man still a child?

1538. When is a letter damp?

1539. When is a well-dressed lion like a weed?

1540. When is the vet busiest?

1541. When is the best time to buy a thermometer?

1542. When do you have acute pain?

1543. When was medicine first mentioned in the Bible?

1544. When does a police dog not look like a police dog?

1545. When is it polite to serve milk in a saucer?

1546. When does a female deer need money?

1547. When the biggest elephant in the world fell into a 30-foot well, how died they get it out?

1548. When does a mouse weigh as much as an elephant?

1549. When is a miniskirt long?

1550. When was beef at its highest?

1551. When is a boat cheapest?

1552. When does a bed grow longer?

1553. When should you charge a new battery?

1554. Why is it hard to make conversation with goats?

1555. What do you make from horns?

1556. When is a man not a man?
1557. When do you go as fast as a racing car?
1558. When do ghosts haunt skyscrapers?
1559. Where can you always find money?
1560. Where are there more nobles than at court?
1561. Where can you find ice-cream in the Bible?
1562. Where was Rosie when the lights went out?
1563. Where do cows go on holiday?
1564. Where do they go dancing in California?
1565. Where does a two-ton gorilla sleep?
1566. Where do tadpoles change into frogs?
1567. Where do gnomes do their shopping?
1568. Where does a general keep his armies?
1569. Where does a dog go when he loses his tail?
1570. Where are whales weighed?
1571. Where did the policeman live?
1572. Where was the Magna Carta signed?
1573. Where do flies go in winter time?
1574. Where do gnomes live?
1575. Where do cars get the most flat tyres?
1576. Where do squirrels go when they have nervous breakdowns?
1577. Where did Caesar go on his thirty-ninth birthday?
1578. Where do you get satisfaction from?
1579. Where does Thursday come before Wednesday?
1580. Where are kings and queens usually crowned?
1581. Where do you take a sick dog?
1582. Where would you find a stupid shoplifter?
1583. Where do bees go for transport?
1584. Where does Tarzan buy his clothes?
1585. Where were chips first fried?
1586. Where did Noah keeps his bees?
1587. Where can you always find diamonds?
1588. Where do all good turkeys go when they die?

1589. Where are all people equally beautiful?
1590. Where are Chinese boats stored?
1591. Where do they put crying children?
1592. Where do you put letters to boys?
1593. Where do baby trees go to school?
1594. Where did the rancher take the sheep?
1595. Where do you end up if you smoke too much?
1596. Where did the three little kittens find their mittens?
1597. Where do blackbirds drink?
1598. Where do ghosts go for fresh air?
1599. Where do trees keep their money?
1600. Where do hogs keep their money?
1601. Where do Eskimos keep their money?
1602. Where do fish keep their money?
1603. Where did Abraham Lincoln live?
1604. Where do children grow?
1605. Where do mummies swim?
1606. Where do fish wash themselves?
1607. Where do tough chickens come from?
1608. Where did King Arthur go for entertainment?
1609. Where can you find cards on a ship?
1610. Where do golfers dance?
1611. Where do flowers come from?
1612. Where do butchers dance?
1613. Which hand should you use to stir tea?
1614. Which is more important, the sun or the moon?
1615. Which American has the biggest family?
1616. Which is more nourishing, a cow or a shooting star?
1617. Which is better, an old ten dollar bill or a new one?
1618. Which key is best for unlocking a tongue?
1619. Which stars are like wicked old men?
1620. Which is better: The house burned down or the house burned up?
1621. Which side of the cup is its handle?

1622. Which tool grows sharper with age?

1623. Which chestnut invaded Britain?

1624. Which cake wanted to rule the world?

1625. Which member of Robin Hood's band was Welsh?

1626. Which King of England invented the fireplace?

1627. Which roof covers the noisiest tenant?

1628. Which word is always pronounced wrongly?

1629. Which is the strongest day of the week?

1630. Which musician had the largest family?

1631. Which has more legs, a horse or no horse?

1632. Which eye gets hit the most?

1633. Which is heavier - a pound of head or a pound of feathers?

1634. What did the wig say as it blew along the street?

1635. Which of your relatives are dependent upon you for a living?

1636. Which burns longer—a wax candle or a tallow candle?

1637. Which animal has wooden legs?

1638. Which two letters of the alphabet have nothing between them?

1639. Which fish feels the most comfortable on ice?

1640. Which bird was allowed to stay at the round table with King Arthur?

1641. Which is greater, six dozen dozen or half a dozen dozen?

1642. What did the traffic lights say to the zebra crossing?

1643. While walking with a young man, a woman was asked who he was. She said, 'His mother is my mother's only child.' Who was the young man?

1644. Who invented the hole in the doughnut?

1645. Who earns a living without doing a day's work?

1646. Who invented spaghetti?

1647. Who is always being let down by his mates?

1648. Who drives all his customers away?

1649. Who gets the sack as soon as he starts work?

1650. Who is strong enough to hold up a car with one hand?

1651. Who were the first gamblers?

1652. Who has the biggest boots in the British Army?

1653. Who invented gunpowder?

1654. Who was the first underwater spy?

1655. Who was Mexico's most famous fat man?

1656. Who won the World Cup in 1920?

1657. Who sailed the Seven Seas looking for rubbish and blubber?

1658. Who invented fire?

1659. Who never gets his hair wet in the shower?

1660. Who settled in the West before anyone else?

1661. Who was older, David or Goliath?

1662. Who is the biggest liar in the world?

1663. Who was the biggest thief in history?

1664. Who wears the smallest hat?

1665. Who was the strongest man in the Bible?

1666. Who has the strongest fingers in the world?

1667. Who is the most musical grandfather you could have?

1668. Who is the fattest female phantom?

1669. Who was the first to have a mobile home?

1670. Why did the cockerel cross the road?

1671. Who makes suits and eats spinach?

1672. Why do kangaroos hate rainy days?

1673. Who is the strongest thief?

1674. Who dares to sit down in front of the Queen with his hat on?

1675. Who earns his living without doing a day's work?

1676. Who often has his friends for lunch?

1677. Who was the first man in space?

1678. Why did the burglar take a bath?

1679. Why were the Dark Ages so dark?

1680. Why was the dentist not interested in his work?

1681. Why did the tortoise beat the hare?

1682. Why did the surveyor take his ruler to bed?

1683. Why do cows wear bells?
1684. Why is Kevin Keegan like a matchstick?
1685. Why couldn't the leopard escape from the zoo?
1686. Why did the old-aged pensioner put wheels on his rocking chair?
1687. Why is a river rich?
1688. Why are there fouls in football?
1689. Why do birds in a nest always agree?
1690. Why is a stupid boy like the Amazon jungle?
1691. Why is a pig like a bottle of ink?
1692. Why is the Isle of Wight a fraud?
1693. Why are tall people lazier than short people?
1694. Why do birds fly south in the winter?
1695. Why is a lazy dog like a hill?
1696. Why did the cowslip?
1697. Why is a banana skin like a pullover?
1698. Why does a barber never shave a man with a wooden leg?
1699. Why did the snowdrop?
1700. Why did the chicken cross the road?
1701. Why was the little boy glad that everyone called him Cyril?
1702. Why do city businessmen carry umbrellas?
1703. Why do we sing Hymns in church and not Hers?
1704. Why did the one-handed man cross the road?
1705. Why is honey scarce in Brighton?
1706. Why are ghosts invisible?
1707. Why is blunt axe like coffee?
1708. Why was the ghost arrested?
1709. Why is a mouse like fresh hay?
1710. Why did the man throw his watch out of the window?
1711. Why is a baby like an old motor-car?
1712. Why did Sir Winston Churchill wear, red, white and blue braces?
1713. Why was the young Scottish owl angry?

1714. Why did the football manager give his team a lighter?

1715. Why is tennis a noisy game?

1716. Why do people laugh up their sleeves?

1717. Why was the cowboy always in trouble?

1718. Why is a rabbit's nose always shiny?

1719. Why do we call money 'bread'?

1720. Why did the nurse creep into the cupboard?

1721. Why is a guidebook like a pair of handcuffs?

1722. Why did the man comb his hair with his toes?

1723. Why is a mouse like fresh grass?

1724. Who is the smallest sailor in the world?

1725. Why is the letter E very lazy?

1726. Why did the priest walk on his hands?

1727. Why is the river said to be lazy?

1728. Why was the kid called "Candy Bar?"

1729. Why did the elephant sit on an orange in front of a synagogue?

1730. Why is everyone tired on 1 April?

1731. Why did the librarian laugh when the borrower insisted on returning the pound note he had left between pages 19 and 20 in the book he had borrowed?

1732. Why is the letter W like a scandalmonger?

1733. Why is the letter F like a banana skin?

1734. Why is the letter G never short?

1735. Why did the cat join the Red Cross.

1736. Why is it wrong to speak of the number 288?

1737. Why is a lady's jumper like a banana peel?

1738. Why is the caterpillar like a greedy boy?

1739. Why is the wick of a candle like the city of Athens?

1740. Why is a short black man like a white man?

1741. Why is a miser like a man who can't remember?

1742. Why is an honest man like a cat burglar, who is at this moment upstairs in your bedroom?

1743. Why is a chicken going along its way like a burglar?

1744. Why is a beehive like a spectator?
1745. Why is Ireland going to be very rich?
1746. Why is a room of married people empty?
1747. Why was Shylock like a diamond when he was ill?
1748. Why are clouds like a man who drives a horse and cart?
1749. Why was the crab arrested?
1750. Why was Christopher Columbus a crook?

Answers

1501. When a car hits you.
1502. Because they are put off till the next day.
1503. When he has a pain in his stomach.
1504. When it makes a spring.
1505. When it's addles (saddled).
1506. Lemonade.
1507. When the water is frozen into ice.
1508. When it isn't made up yet.
1509. When it reaches the bottom.
1510. On a clock.
1511. When he's a robust yeller.
1512. 'I is the letter after H'.
1513. Gets wet.
1514. During the day, because when the sun shines everything is brighter.
1515. When it turns into a garage.
1516. When it has just one copper in it.
1517. Let's spin a yarn together.
1518. Drainpipe trousers.
1519. 'Madam, I'm Adam.'
1520. When their time is up.
1521. The last.
1522. When they make 22.
1523. When it's a skylight.
1524. After a bumpy plane trip....
1525. When it's a-jar.
1526. When it's a baby tiger.
1527. When it's driven.
1528. When it turns over a new leaf.
1529. When it is a shamrock.
1530. Iron ones would rust.
1531. When the bed won't come to you.
1532. When it's taut.
1533. The bathtub.
1534. When it can't bear you.
1535. When it is full.
1536. When it's ticking (sticking) there.
1537. When he is a miner (minor).
1538. When it has postage due (dew).

1539. When he's a dandelion (dandy lion).

1540. When it rains cats and dogs.

1541. In the winter, because then it is lower.

1542. When you own a very pretty window.

1543. When Moses received the two tablets.

1544. When it is an undercover agent.

1545. When you feed the cat.

1546. When she doesn't have a buck.

1547. Wet.

1548. When the scale is broken.

1549. When a midget wears it.

1550. When the cow jumped over the moon.

1551. When it is a sail (sale) boat.

1552. At night, because two feet are added to it.

1553. When you can't pay cash.

1554. They are always butting in.

1555. Hornaments.

1556. When he turns into an alley.

1557. When you are in it.

1558. When they are in high spirits.

1559. In the dictionary.

1560. In the library. All the books have titles.

1561. At the walls of the Jericho.

1562. In the dark.

1563. Moo York.

1564. San Frandisco.

1565. Anywhere he wants to.

1566. In the croakroom.

1567. At the British Gnome Stores.

1568. Up his sleevies.

1569. To a re-tailer.

1570. At a whale weigh station.

1571. Nine mine nine Let's-Be avenue.

1572. At the bottom.

1573. To the glassworks to be turned into blue-bottles.

1574. Gnome Sweet Gnome.

1575. When there is a fork in the road.

1576. To the nuthouse.

1577. Into his fortieth year.

1578. A satis-factory.

1579. In a dictionary.

1580. On the head.

1581. To the dogtor.

1582. Squashed under Tesco's.

1583. The buzz-shop.

1584. At a jungle sale.

1585. In Greece.

1586. In the ark hives.

1587. In a pack of cards.

1588. To oven.

1589. In the dark.

1590. In a junkyard.

1591. In a bawl (ball) park.

1592. In a mail (male) box.

1593. To a tree nursery.

1594. To the bah-bah (barber) shop.

1595. Coffin (coughin').
1596. In the Yellow Pages?
1597. At a crowbar.
1598. To the sea ghost (coast).
1599. In branch banks.
1600. In piggy banks.
1601. In snowbanks.
1602. In river banks.
1603. "I have his Gettysburg Address right here!"
1604. In a kindergarten.
1605. In the Dead Sea.
1606. In the river basin.
1607. From hard-boiled eggs.
1608. To a nightclub (knight club).
1609. On the deck.
1610. At the golf ball.
1611. The stalk (stork) brings them.
1612. At the meatball.
1613. Neither. It is better to use a spoon.
1614. The moon. It shines when it is dark, but the sun shines when it is light anyway.
1615. George Washington—because he was the father of his country.
1616. A shooting star, because it is meteor (meatier).
1617. Any old ten dollar bill is better than a new one.
1618. Whisky.
1619. Those that sin till late (Scintillate)
1620. Neither: they are both bad.

1621. Outside.
1622. The tongue.
1623. William the Conker.
1624. Attila the Bun.
1625. Rhyl Scarlet.
1626. Alfred the Grate.
1627. The roof of your mouth.
1628. The one that's spelled W R O N G L Y.
1629. Sunday, because all the rest are weekdays.
1630. Beethoven - he was known as the father of German music.
1631. No horse. A horse has four legs but no horse has six legs.
1632. A bullseye.
1633. They both weigh the same.
1634. I'm off my head!
1635. Your aunts, uncles and cousins, for without U they could not exist.
1636. Neither: they both burn shorter.
1637. A timber wolf.
1638. N and P—they have O between them.
1639. A skate.
1640. The knightingale.
1641. Six dozen dozen, it is 864, while the other is 72.
1642. Don't look—I'm changing.
1643. Her son.
1644. A fresh-air fiend.
1645. A night-porter.
1646. An Italian who used his noodle.

1647. A deep-sea diver.

1648. A taxi-driver.

1649. A postman.

1650. A policeman.

1651. Adam and Eve, 'cos they had a pair 'o dice (Paradise).

1652. The soldier with the biggest feet.

1653. A lady who wanted guns to look pretty.

1654. James Pond.

1655. Pauncho Villa.

1656. No one - the first World Cup competition was held in 1930.

1657. Binbag the Whaler.

1658. Some bright spark....

1659. A bald man.

1660. The sun.

1661. David must have been because he rocked Goliath to sleep.

1662. A rodeo man, because he is always trying to throw the bull.

1663. Atlas, because he held up the whole world.

1664. A narrow-minded person.

1665. Jonah. Even the whale couldn't keep him down.

1666. A miser because he is always pinching pennies.

1667. One who fiddles with his beard.

1668. The ghostess with the mostest.

1669. A turtle.

1670. To show he wasn't chicken.

1671. Popeye the Tailorman.

1672. Because their children have to play indoors.

1673. A shoplifter.

1674. Her chauffeur.

1675. A night watchman.

1676. A cannibal.

1677. The man in the moon.

1678. So he could make a clean getaway.

1679. They had more knights in those days.

1680. He found the drilling boring.

1681. Because nothing goes faster than Shell.

1682. 'Cos he wanted to see how long he would sleep.

1683. Their horns don't work.

1684. 'Cos he strikes from the edge of the box.

1685. 'Cos he was always spotted.

1686. 'Cos he wanted to rock 'n'roll.

1687. Because it has two banks.

1688. Because there are ducks in cricket.

1689. Because they don't want to fall out.

1690. They're both dense.

1691. Because it keeps going into the pen and then running out.

1692. Because it has Fresh-water you can't drink, Cowes you can't milk, Needles you can't thread and Newport you can't bottle.

1693. Because they're longer in bed.

1694. Because it's too far to walk.

1695. Because it's slow pup (slope up).

1696. 'Cos it saw the bullrush.

1697. Because it's easy to slip on.

1698. Because he always uses a razor.

1399. 'Cos it heard the crocuss!

1700. For fowl (foul) purposes.

1701. 'Cos that was his name.

1702. 'Cos umbrellas can't walk.

1703. Because they all finish with Amen and not A-women.

1704. To get to the second-hand shop.

1705. Because there's only one B in Brighton.

1706. 'Cos they wear see-through clothes.

1707. Because both have to be ground.

1708. Because he hadn't got a haunting licence.

1709. Both make ma mad.

1710. To see time fly.

1711. Because both have a rattle.

1712. To keep his red, white and blue trousers up.

1713. Because his mother wouldn't let him hoot at night.

1714. 'Cos they kept losing their matches.

1715. 'Cos when you play it you have to raise a racket.

1716. Because that's where their funny-bone is.

1717. 'Cos he couldn't stop horsing around.

1718. 'Cos it keeps its powder puff at the wrong end.

1719. 'Cos everybody 'kneads' it.

1720. So as not to wake the sleeping-pills.

1721. Because it is for tourists (two wrists).

1722. To make two ends meet.

1723. Because the cattle (cat'll) eat it.

1724. The one who sleeps on his watch.

1725. Because it lies in the middle of bed.

1726. Because it was Palm Sunday.

1727. Because it never leaves its bed.

1728. Because he was half nuts.

1729. Because it just wanted to see the Jews (juice) come out.

1730. Because they just had a march of 31 days.

1731. Pages 19 and 20 are the sides of the same leaf.

1732. Because it makes ill-will.

1733. They both make all fall.

1734. Because it always ends 'long'.

1735. It wanted to be a first-aid kit.

1736. Because it is too gross (two gross = 144 x 2).

1737. Because they both are easy to slip on.

1738. They both make the butterfly (butter fly).

1739. Because they are both in the middle of Greece (grease).

1740. Because he is not at all black (not a tall black).

1741. They are both for getting (forgetting).

1742. They are both above doing a bad action.

1743. Because it is a fowl proceeding (foul).

1744. It is a beholder (bee holder).

1745. Because its capital is always Dublin (Doubling).

1746. Because there is not a single person in it.

1747. Because he was a Jew-ill (Jewel).

1748. They both hold reins (rains).

1749. 'Cos he was always pinching things.

1750. 'Cos he double-crossed the Atlantic.

Riddles 1751-2000

1751. Why is there no tug-o-war match between England and France?

1752. Why do idiots eat biscuits?

1753. Why do bears wear fur coats?

1754. What's the route through Khyber called?

1755. Why did the man take a pencil to bed?

1756. Why do white sheep eat more grass than black sheep?

1757. Why doesn't the sea ever fall into space?

1758. Why are cooks cruel?

1759. How does a horse have six legs?

1760. Why did the school-leaver not want to work in the fabrics firm?

1761. Why should you never gossip in fields?

1762. Why did Kojak throw away the keys?

1763. Why are Frenchmen cannibals?

1764. Why is there always a wall round a gravevard?

1765. Why did the Red Indian put a bucket over his head?

1766. Why does the giraffe have a long neck?

1767. Why did the owl make everyone laugh?

1768. Why do cows have horns?

1769. Why did Tiny throw the butter out of the window?

1770. Why did Nelson wear a three-cornered hat?

1771. Why does Batman search for worms?

1772. Why is the sand wet?

1773. Why did the tap run?

1774. Why did the biscuit cry?

1775. Why did the one-eyed chicken cross the road?

1776. Why did the farmer drive over his potato field with a steamroller?

1777. Why are 4,840 square yards like a bad tooth?

1778. Why does a young lady need the letter Y?

1779. Why are your tonsils unhappy?

1780. Why is it dangerous to put the letter 'M' into the fridge?

1781. Why are whist players aggressive?

1782. Why did the milkmaid sit down?

1783. Why is the sea always restless?

1784. Why does a Scoutmaster have to take a lot of rubbish?

1785. Why did the apple turn over?

1786. Why is the letter A like a flower?

1787. Why can the world never come to an end?

1788. Why did the weeping willow weep?

1789. Why can't a car play football?

1790. Why is the letter T an island?

1791. Why is perfume always very obedient?

1792. Why did the hedgehog cross the road?

1793. Why did the Communist chicken cross the road?

1794. Why did the pop singer go to the barber?

1795. Why is the sea so suspicious?

1796. Why did King Kong climb up the Empire State Building?

1797. Why is Batman a coward?

1798. Why is a lion in the desert like Christmas?

1799. Why do actors hang around snooker halls?

1800. Why were the United Nations worried when a waiter dropped his tray?

1801. Why should you always have plenty of clocks in the house?

1802. Why did the antelope?

1803. Why is the Eiffel Tower so called?

1804. Why was Cleopatra so cantankerous?

1805. Why did the Lone Ranger rake a hammer to bed?

1806. Why did the scientist have his phone cut off?

1807. Why are dentists unhappy?
1808. Why is your nose in the middle of your face?
1809. Why are there so few lady pilots?
1810. Why is Buckingham Palace cheap to maintain?
1811. Why is an airplane like a confidence trickster?
1812. Why did the cat cross the road?
1813. Why are teachers special?
1814. Why was the Boy Scout dizzy?
1815. Why are bakers invariably good people?
1816. Why did the bus stop?
1817. Why did the train go 'Ouch!'?
1818. Why is a chemistry lesson like a worm in a cornfield?
1819. Why did the rabbit cross the road?
1820. Why was the baby raised on cat's milk?
1821. Why did the stupid postman get the sack?
1822. Why did the simpleton bury his car battery?
1823. Why should Elijah's parents be remembered by all business people?
1824. Why are you taking that steel wool home?
1825. Why did the fireman wear red trousers?
1826. Why couldn't the sailors play cards?
1827. Why did the orange stop rolling down the hill?
1828. Why couldn't Cinderella go to the ball?
1829. Why did the bald-headed man look of the window?
1830. Why are adults boring?
1831. Why did Henry VIII have so many wives?
1832. Why do some women wear curlers at night?
1833. Why are goldfish gold?
1834. Why is the letter P like a Roman emperor?
1835. Why is a Christmas pudding like the ocean?
1836. Why is it more dangerous to go to the woods in springtime?
1837. Why do birds fly south?
1838. Why does the giraffe have such a long neck?

1839. Why did the butterfly flutter by?

1840. Why did Moses have to be hidden quickly when he was a baby?

1841. Why are first class footballers like accomplished musicians?

1842. Why did the man laugh after his operation?

1843. Why are your nose and your handkerchief deadly enemies?

1844. Why are postmen clever people?

1845. Why will telly never take the place of newspapers?

1846. Why wasn't the elephant allowed on the aeroplane?

1847. Why is a poor joke like an unsharpened pencil?

1848. Why are heavy drinkers like heavy showers?

1849. Why is there no such thing as a whole day?

1850. Why is it silly to buy coal?

1851. Why is a man who marries twice like the captain of a ship?

1852. Why was the mother flea so sad?

1853. Why is it that there's not a moment that we can call our own?

1854. Why are waiters good at sums?

1855. Why is a tall building dangerous?

1856. Why did the baker stop baking bread?

1857. Why was the inventor of the safety match so pleased?

1858. Why is a black chicken smarter than a white one?

1859. Why is the Prince of Wales like a cloudy day?

1860. Why is it a mistake to put on a shoe?

1861. Why should a greedy man wear a tartan vest?

1862. Why should you not swim in the river at Paris?

1863. Why did the boy wear two suits to the fancy dress party?

1864. Why do you always start to walk with the right foot first?

1865. Why shouldn't you tell secrets when there's a clock in the room?

1866. Why is a penny like a policeman?

1867. Why is a herring like a cemetery?

1868. Why do we dress baby girls in pink and baby boys in blue?
1869. Why do surgeons wear masks during operations?
1870. Why does your sense of touch suffer if you are ill?
1871. Why did the man hit the clock?
1872. What did the mother bee say to the baby bees?
1873. Why did the lobster blush?
1874. Why can't anyone stay angry long with an actress?
1875. Why would a sixth sense be a handicap?
1876. Why is a week-old loaf like a mouse running into a hole?
1877. Why do you always find something in the last place you look?
1878. Why wouldn't the parrot talk to the Chinaman?
1879. Why is a girl extravagant with her clothes?
1880. Why is a warm day bad for an icicle's character?
1881. Why does the Indian wear feathers in his hair?
1882. Why is a bad cold a great humiliation?
1883. Why does the stork stand on one leg only?
1884. Why is a doctor less likely to be upset on an ocean voyage?
1885. Why should you not upset a cannibal?
1886. Why do women make good post-office workers?
1887. Why did the man keep a ruler on his newspaper?
1888. Why is a clock like a river?
1889. Why is waiting on the telephone like doing a trapeze act?
1890. Why is the theatre such a sad place?
1891. Why will the radio not take the place of newspapers?
1892. What games do cows like playing?
1893. Why do some people press the lift button with the thumb and others with the forefinger?
1894. Why is a crossword puzzle like a quarrel?
1895. Why is a pretty girl like an expensive mirror?
1896. Why is a garden like a story?
1897. Why did the Romans build straight roads?
1898. Why can't a deaf man be sent to prison?
1899. Why do lions eat raw meat?

1900. Why is a poor friend better than a rich one?

1901. Why were the elephants thrown out of the swimming pool?

1902. Why is a pig in the house like a house on fire?

1903. Why is a tramp like a balloon?

1904. Why is a Viking like a cavalry officer?

1905. Why is mayonnaise never ready?

1906. Why is Westminster Abbey like a fireplace?

1907. Why is a single person like borrowed money?

1908. Why can't it rain for two nights in a row?

1909. Why did the man get a set of tools?

1910. Why would a squeaking shoe be a good song-writer?

1911. Why shouldn't you tell a joke while you are ice skating?

1912. Why did the jam roll?

1913. Why are goalkeepers thrifty?

1914. Why is the letter S like thunder?

1915. Why is Derbyshire a good place for pet dogs?

1916. Why did the butcher put bells on his scale?

1917. Why did the farmer feed money to his cows?

1918. Why did the man climb up to the chandelier?

1919. Why do you go to bed?

1920. Why are the days long in summer and short in winter?

1921. Why are dentists artistic?

1922. Why are mosquitoes annoying?

1923. Why is a lady's belt like a dustcart?

1924. Why did the mad chef catch the lazy cow?

1925. Why is a rifle like a lazy worker?

1926. Why did the pigeon fly over the racecourse?

1927. Why is a piano like an eye?

1928. Why is a field of grass older than you?

1929. What happens if you watch too many Mickey Mouse movies?

1930. Why did the girl sit on her watch?

1931. Why is O the only vowel that is sounded?

1932. Why is a race at a circus like a big fire?
1933. Why are a fat man's braces like a big traffic jam?
1934. Why doesn't the piano work?
1935. Why is a bride always out of luck on her wedding day?
1936. Why does a man's hair turn grey before his moustache?
1937. Why did the gardener throw roses into the burning building?
1938. Why is an empty purse always the same?
1939. Why would a compliment from a chicken be an insult?
1940. Why is a lame dog like a boy adding six and seven?
1941. Why did Moses lose the race?
1942. Why couldn't the mountain climber call for help?
1943. Why did the wife understand her invisible husband so well?
1944. Why did the old lady who mended basins go crazy?
1945. Why is an underground coal miner like a beautician?
1946. Why do cows wear bells?
1947. Why did the greedy boy pick all the white meat off the chicken?
1948. Why are policeman like the days of man?
1949. Why is it easy to weigh fish?
1950. Why is a manicurist sure to get rich?
1951. Why is food that does not agree with you like a cook's apron?
1952. Why would a drummer in a swing band make a good policeman?
1953. Why did Robin Hood rob the rich?
1954. Why was Winston Churchill buried in Oxfordshire?
1955. Why is snow different from Sunday?
1956. Why is a shoemaker like a clergyman?
1957. Why did the spy pull the sheets over his head?
1958. Why is group of convicts like a deck of cards?
1959. Why did Sarah marry the acrobat?
1960. Why is a duke like a book?

1961. Why did the man ring up the dentist?

1962. Why are blacksmiths undesirable citizens?

1963. Why are British soldiers not to have bayonets any longer?

1964. Why do they call it a libel suit?

1965. What do you do if you see two snails fighting?

1966. Why was the dog chasing his tail?

1967. Why do ducks look so sad?

1968. Why is your heart like a policeman?

1969. Why do nudists have plenty of time to spare?

1970. Why did the silly boy go onto the road with his bread and butter?

1971. Why is a railway patriotic?

1972. Why were the man's socks full of holes?

1973. Why does the butcher's wife always keep the books?

1974. Why is a ferryboat like a good rule?

1975. Why did the girl tear the calendar?

1976. Why did the man have to repair the horn of his car?

1977. Why are money and secrets both alike?

1978. Why is the letter K like a pig's tail?

1979. Why were the elephants the last animals to leave the Ark?

1980. Why does a dog wag his tail?

1981. Why did the girl call herself an experienced actress?

1982. Why do bees hum?

1983. Why is the letter D like a wedding ring?

1984. Why is a river a good place for getting money?

1985. Why is Buckingham Palace the cheapest palace ever built?

1986. Why are oranges like bells?

1987. Why is a pig's tail like 5 a.m.?

1988. Why is a pony like a person with a sore throat?

1989. Why is a newborn baby like a storm?

1990. Why do two fivers make a singer?

1991. Why did the boy put his bed in the fireplace?

1992. Why can two very thin people not become good friends?

1993. Why does a cow go over a hill?

1994. What happened when the zoo pandas had a fight?
1995. Why is a mirror like a resolution?
1996. Why did the man put a clock under his desk?
1997. Why is an MP like somebody queuing outside a cinema?
1998. Why is a pig the most amazing animal in the farmyard?
1999. Why is U the merriest letter?
2000. Why are boarding housekeepers called landladies?

Answers

1751. 'Cos no-one can find a rope twenty-six miles long!
1752. Because they're crackers.
1753. They'd look silly in plastic macs.
1754. Pass.
1755. To draw the curtains...I'd tell you another joke about a pencil but it hasn't any point.
1756. 'Cos there are more of them.
1757. It's tide.
1758. 'Cos they beat eggs and batter fish.
1759. 'Cos it has forelegs in front and two behind.
1760. 'Cos she was too young to dye.
1761. 'Because corn has ears, potatoes have eyes and beanstalk.
1762. 'Cos he didn't have any locks.
1763. 'Cos they like eating Froggies' legs.
1764. 'Cos people are dying to get in.

1765. 'Cos he wanted to be a pailface.
1766. 'Cos he can't stand the smell of his feet.
1767. 'Cos he was a hoot!
1768. 'Cos their bells don't work.
1769. 'Cos he wanted to see a butterfly.
1770. To keep his three-cornered head warm.
1771. To feed his Robin.
1772. Because the seaweed.
1773. 'Cos it saw the kitchen sink.
1774. 'Cos his mother was a wafer so long.
1775. To get to the Bird's Eye shop.
1776. 'Cos he wanted mashed potatoes.
1777. Because it's an acre.
1778. 'Cos without it she'd be a young lad.
1779. 'Cos they're always down in the mouth.
1780. Because it changes ice into mice.

1781. 'Cos they often lead with a club.

1782. 'Cos she couldn't stand milking.

1783. 'Cos it's got so many rocks in its bed.

1784. Because he's a Skip.

1785. 'Cos it saw the cheese roll.

1786. 'Cos a B is always after it.

1787. 'Cos it's round.

1788. 'Cos it saw the pine tree pine.

1789. 'Cos it's only got one boot.

1790. 'Cos it's in the middle of the water.

1791. 'Cos it is scent wherever it goes.

1792. To see his flatmate.

1793. 'Cos it was a Rhode Island Red.

1794. He couldn't stand his hair any longer.

1795. 'Cos it's been crossed so often.

1796. To catch a plane.

1797. 'Cos he's frightened of a duck.

1798. 'Cos of its Sandy Claws.

1799. 'Cos that's where they are sure to get some cues.

1800. 'Cos it was the fall of Turkey, China was broken and Greece was overthrown!

1801. Because time is precious.

1802. Nobody gnu.

1803. 'Cos from the top you sure get an eye-full!

1804. She was Queen of denial.

1805. So he could hit the hay.

1806. 'Cos he wanted to win the Nobel prize.

1807. 'Cos they're always looking down in the mouth.

1808. 'Cos it's the scenter (centre).

1809. 'Cos no girl wants to be a plane woman!

1810. 'Cos it's run for a sovereign.

1811. They both have no visible means of support.

1812. 'Cos it was staped to the chicken...(ugh!)

1813. 'Cos they're in a class of their own.

1814. He'd done too many good turns.

1815. 'Cos they earn an honest crust.

1816. 'Cos it saw the zebra crossing.

1817. 'Cos it had a tender behind.

1818. The both go in one ear and out the other.

1819. To show his girlfriend he had guts.

1820. 'Cos it was a baby kitten.

1821. To put his stupid letters in.

1822. 'Cos the mechanic told him it was dead.

1823. Because they made a prophet.

1824. 'I'm going to knit myself a car.'

1825. His blue ones were at the cleaners.

1826. 'Cos the captain was standing on the deck.

1827. It ran out of juice.

1828. 'Cos it had a puncture.

1829. To get some fresh air.

1830. 'Cos they're groan-ups.

1831. He liked to chop and change.

1832. So they can wake up curly in the morning.

1833. So they won't go rusty.

1834. Because it is near O.

1835. It's full of currants.

1836. Because in the spring the grass has blades, the flowers have pistils, the leaves shoot, the cowslips about, and the bullrush is out.

1837. Because it's too far to walk.

1838. Because its head is so far from its body.

1839. Because it saw the dragonfly drink the flagon dry.

1840. Because it was a 'rush' job to save him.

1841. Because they are very good players.

1842. The doctor put him in stitches.

1843. Because they can't meet without coming to blows.

1844. Because they are men of letters.

1845. You can't swat flies with a telly.

1846. Because its trunk was too big to fit under the seat.

1847. Because it has no point.

1848. Because they usually begin with little drops.

1849. Because every day begins by breaking.

1850. Because instead of going to the buyer, it goes to the cellar.

1851. Because he was a second mate.

1852. Because her children were going to the dogs.

1853. Because the minutes are not hours.

1854. Because they know their tables.

1855. Because it has a lot of flaws (floors) in it.

1856. Because he wasn't making enough dough.

1857. Because it was a striking success.

1858. Because a black chicken can lay a white egg, but a white chicken can't lay a black one.

1859. Because he is likely to reign.

1860. Because you're putting your foot in it.

1861. To keep a check on his stomach.

1862. If you did you would be in Seine.

1863. He went as twins.

1864. Because when you move one foot, the other is always left behind.

1865. Because time will tell.
1866. They're both coppers.
1867. Because it is full of bones.
1868. Because they can't dress themselves.
1869. So that if they make a mistake, no one will know who did it.
1870. Because you don't feel well.
1871. Because the clock struck first.
1872. Either behive yourselves or buzz off.
1873. Because it saw the salad dressing.
1874. Because she always makes up.
1875. Because it would be a new sense.
1876. Because you can see it's stale.
1877. Because when you find it, you stop looking.
1878. Because he only spoke pigeon English.
1879. When she has a new dress she wears it out the first day.
1880. Because it turns into an eavesdropper.
1881. To keep his wigwam.
1882. Because it can bring a proud man to his sneeze.
1883. If he lifted it, he would fall down.
1884. Because he is accustomed to see sickness.
1885. Because if you do, you might find yourself in hot water.

1886. Because they know how to manage the mails.
1887. Because he wanted to get the story straight.
1888. Because it won't run for long without winding.
1889. Because you have to hang on.
1890. Because all the seats are in line.
1891. You can't light the fire with a radio.
1892. Moo-sical games.
1893. To signal the lift.
1894. Because one word leads to another.
1895. Because she is a good looking lass.
1896. They both have plots.
1897. Because they didn't want to drive their horses round the bend.
1898. Because you can't condemn a man without a hearing.
1899. Because they don't know how to cook.
1900. Because a friend in need is a friend indeed.
1901. Because they couldn't hold their trunks up.
1902. Because the sooner you put it out, the better.
1903. Because he has no visible means of support.
1904. Because he's a Norseman.
1905. Because it is always dressing.
1906. Because it contains the ashes of the great.

1907. Because he is alone.

1908. Because there is a day between.

1909. Everyone said he had a screw loose.

1910. Because it has music in its sole.

1911. Because the ice might crack up.

1912. Because it saw the apple turnover.

1913. Because saving is their job.

1914. Because it makes our milk sour milk.

1915. Because it is the peak (peke) district.

1916. Because he wanted to jingle all the way (weigh).

1917. He wanted rich milk.

1918. He was a light sleeper.

1919. Because the bed will not come to you.

1920. Because heat expands things, and cold contracts them.

1921. Because they are good at drawing teeth.

1922. Because they get under your skin.

1923. Because it goes round and round and gathers the waist.

1924. He liked to see the meat loaf.

1925. Because they can both get fired.

1926. Because it wanted to have a flutter on the horses.

1927. Because they are both closed when their lids are down.

1928. Because it is past-ur-age.

1929. You'll have Disney spells.

1930. She wanted to be on time.

1931. Because all the others are in audible.

1932. Because the heat is in tents.

1933. Because they are both big hold-ups.

1934. Because it only knows how to play.

1935. Because she never marries the best man.

1936. Because it's older.

1937. He heard that flowers grew better in hot houses.

1938. Because there's never any change in it.

1939. Because it would be fowl language.

1940. Because he puts down three and carries one.

1941. Because the Lord told him to come forth.

1942. Because he was hanging on by his teeth.

1943. Because she could see right through him.

1944. She was around cracked pots too long.

1945. Because they are both face workers.

1946. Because their horns won't work.

1947. To make a clean breast of it.

1948. Because they are numbered.

1949. Because they have their own scales.

1950. Because she makes money hand over first.

1951. Because it goes against the stomach.

1952. Because he's used to pounding the beat.

1953. Because the poor didn't have any money.

1954. Because he was dead.

1955. Because it can fall on any day of the week.

1956. Both try to save soles.

1957. He was an undercover agent.

1958. Because there is a knave in every suit.

1959. Because he was head over heels in love with her.

1960. Because he has a title.

1961. Because he was aching to meet him.

1962. Because they forge and steel.

1963. Because they are long enough.

1964. Because you're liable to win and you're liable to lose.

1965. Let them slug it out.

1966. He was trying for both ends to meet.

1967. When they preen their feathers they get down in the mouth.

1968. Because it has a regular beat.

1969. Because they have nothing on.

1970. He was looking for the traffic jam.

1971. Because it is bound to the country with the strongest ties.

1972. Because he didn't give a darn.

1973. Because the business is a joint affair.

1974. Because it works both ways.

1975. Because she wanted to take a month off.

1976. Because it didn't give a hoot.

1977. They are both hard to keep.

1978. Because it is the end of pork.

1979. They had to pack their trunks.

1980. Because no one else will wag it for him.

1981. She broke her leg and was in a cast for six months.

1982. Because they don't know the words.

1983. Because you cannot be wed without it.

1984. There is a bank on either side.

1985. Because it was built for one sovereign and furnished for another.

1986. You can peel both of them.

1987. They are both twirly (too early).

1988. Because they are both a little ho (a) rse.

1989. Because it begins with a squall.

1990. Because together they make a tenner (tenor).

1991. So he could sleep like a log.

1992. They must always be slight acquaintances.

1993. Because she can't go under it.

1994. Panda-monium.

1995. Because it is so easily broken.

1996. He decided to work overtime.

1997. Because he stands in order to get a seat.

1998. Because first he is killed, then he is cured.

1999. Because it it always in the midst of fun.

2000. Because they charge the earth.

Riddles 2001-2214

2001. What do sheikhs use to hide from their enemies?

2002. Why is a cash register like someone who can't pay his bills?

2003. Why is an optician like a teacher?

2004. Why are birds poor?

2005. Why are scales like road-maps?

2006. Why is the food one eats on a tossing ship like a difficult conundrum?

2007. Why is the condition of a sick man improved by having won the Derby?

2008. Why do bull dogs have flat faces?

2009. Why is Madame Tussaud's a disagreeable place to visit?

2010. Why was the man standing on the railway bridge with a rod and line?

2011. Why did it take three Boy Scouts to take the old lady across the street?

2012. Why did the waiter look grumpy?

2013. Why did the tightrope walker carry his bankbook?

2014. Why should you tickle a mule?

2015. Why has a shoemaker great powers of endurance?

2016. Why does a policeman's coat have brass buttons?

2017. Why is the nose on your face like the V in civility?

2018. Why was the young lady angry to receive a burning kiss from her boyfriend?

2019. Why is a volcano like an irritable person?

2020. Why is a lie like a wig?

2021. Why is the Pacific like an idea?

2022. Why did the chauffeur never have any trouble with 'back seat' drivers?

2023. Why did the boy's mother knit him three socks for Christmas?

2024. Why was Solomon so in love with his 999th wife?

2025. Why did the orchestra have bad manners?

2026. Why is a Member of Parliament like a shrimp?

2027. Why is a chef to a royal household like a bucketful of coal?

2028. Why did the doctor give up his practice?

2029. Why is a man who's always complaining the easiest man to satisfy?

2030. Why did the twenty-stone girl marry the thirty-stone man?

2031. Why is an old car like a baby playing?

2032. Why shouldn't you believe a person in bed?

2033. Why couldn't the young witch write a decent letter?

2034. Why is twice ten like twice eleven?

2035. Why was Mr. Smith not pleased to bump into his old friend?

2036. Why would someone in jail want to catch chickenpox?

2037. Why was there no standing on top of the bus?

2038. Why were the girl's holiday snaps not ready when she called for them?

2039. Why do Irish farmers wear capes?

2040. Why is an onion like a ringing bell?

2041. Why is a lucky gambler a charming fellow?

2042. Why is a song by a very bad singer like an old man's head?

2043. Why did Mrs. Newrich buy a Ming vase?

2044. Why is a thief like a thermometer on a hot day?

2045. Why are men going bald at an older age these days?

2046. Why can't you remember the last tooth that you had extracted?

2047. Why does a bald-headed man have no use for keys?

2048. Why did the girl keep running round her bed?

2049. Why did the golfer wear two pairs of trousers?

2050. 32 white horses upon a red hill.
They stamp and chomp and they stand still.
Who are they?

2051. Why was the worker fired from his job at the bed-factory?

2052. Why are country people smarter than town people?

2053. Why is a new baby like a diamond?

2054. Why was the chicken sick?

2055. Why is a cannon like a lady's make-up case?

2056. Why are the fifteenth and fourteenth letters of the alphabet more important than all the others?

2057. Why are a star and an old barn both alike?

2058. 10, 9, 8, 7, 6, 5, 4, 3, 2, 1. Now tell me the time.

2059. Why do windows squeak when you open them?

2060. Why is an acrobat like a whisky glass?

2061. Why is the letter R essential to friendship?

2062. Why do you brush your hair before going to bed?

2063. Why did the silly boy try to lock his father in the fridge?

2064. Why is measles like a steel trap?

2065. Why does a chief wear a tall white hat?

2066. Why was young Sam a born leader?

2067. You've heard of a flying fox - what is a flying dog?

2068. You never catch cold going up in an elevator. True or false?

2069. Why should a sailor know best what is going on in the moon?

2070. Why is a greedy man like one with a short memory?

2071. Why are storytellers strange creatures?

2072. Why is dancing like new milk?

2073. Why didn't the man believe the sardine's story?

2074. Why are doctors good-natured?

2075. Why did the girl like her work in the towel factory?

2076. Why was Shakespeare able to write so well?

2077. Why is a heavy fall of snow easily understood?

2078. Why should a fainting lady have more than one doctor?

2079. Why is a trampoline act a tricky way of earning a living?

2080. Why does a watermelon have so much water in it?

2081. Why is a tonic like an ambulance?

2082. Why did the fireplace call the doctor?

2083. Why is it vulgar to sing by yourself?

2084. Why are pianos noble?

2085. Why is a busybody like tallow?

2086. Why did the mother put her baby on the record-player?

2087. Why do portraits of George Washington always show him standing?

2088. Why does Father Time wear sticking plaster?

2089. Why are spiders like tops?

2090. Why did the sleepy boy throw away his alarm clock?

2091. Why did the small boy stamp on his letter?

2092. Why did the dog run round in circles?

2093. Why are playing cards like wolves?

2094. Why are sheep like pubs?

2095. Why is Saturday night important to Julius's girlfriend?

2096. Why did the motorist drive his car in reverse?

2097. Why is the wheel of a motor car like a lazy person?

2098. Why may we doubt the existence of the Blarney Stone?

2099. Why is a guitar like a turkey being made ready for the oven?

2100. Why did the little girl put her head on the piano?

2101. Why might a man with indigestion hope for a long life?

2102. Why did the spy speak in a whisper?

2103. Why did the waiter stamp on his customer's beef burger?

2104. Why must a dishonest man stay indoors?

2105. Why is a false friend like the letter P?

2106. Why should a clock never be put upstairs?

2107. Why was Cinderella thrown out of the football team?

2108. Why is a seascape artist like a large ship?

2109. Why can you always believe a ruler?

2110. Why are waiters always willing to learn?

2111. Why is coffee like a dull knife?

2112. Why did the boy put his trousers on backwards?

2113. You can take away my first letter, and my second letter. You can take away all my letters, and yet I remain the same. What am I?

2114. Why is the letter G like the sun?

2115. Why did the pretty schoolteacher marry the caretaker?

2116. Why should you leave your watch home when you take an airplane?

2117. Why did the nutty kid throw a bucket of water out of the window?

2118. Why did the lady throw a glass of water out of the window?

2119. Why do people always say to you, "A penny for your thoughts"?

2120. Why did the kid avoid the cemetery?

2121. Why does a mother carry her baby?

2122. Why did the reporter put a flashlight into his mouth?

2123. Why do firemen wear red suspenders?

2124. Why does a pencil seem heavy when you write with it for a long time?

2125. Why do we buy clothes?

2126. Why is a toupee like a secret?

2127. Why shouldn't you put grease on your hair the night before a test?

2128. Why can't a mind reader read your mind?

2129. Why did the window pane blush?

2130. Why did the kid keep his shirt on when he took a bath?

2131. Why did the cowboy ride his horse?

2132. Why was the boy's suit rusty?

2133. Why was the horse all charged up?

2134. Why did the ocean roar?

2135. Why are pants always too short?

2136. Why was the girl named Sugar?

2137. Why don't bananas ever get lonely?

2138. Why doesn't Sweden export cattle?

2139. Why is a barefoot boy like an Eskimo?

2140. Why do ships use knots instead of miles?

2141. Why did the lady hold her ears when she passed the chickens?

2142. Why is a shirt with 8 buttons so interesting?

2143. Why was the Lone Ranger poor?

2144. Why did the tree need less sunshine?

2145. Why was the little horse unhappy?

2146. Why is an inexpensive dog a bad watchdog?

2147. Why did the germ cross the microscope?

2148. Why do your eyes look different when you come from an eye doctor?

2149. Why did the secretary cut her fingers off?

2150. Why are doctors stingy?

2151. Why shouldn't you make jokes about a fat person?

2152. Why did the farmer take the cow to the vet?

2153. Why can't a very thin person stand up straight?

2154. Why is a fishing hook like the measles?

2155. Why is Congress like a cold?

2156. Why did the invisible mother take her invisible child to the doctor?

2157. Why did the kid put his hand in the fuse box when the weather got hot?

2158. Why is a horse with a sore throat twice as sick as any other animal?

2159. Why did the man hit his hand with a hammer?

2160. Why did the mother ghost take her ghost child to the doctor?

2161. Why is it dangerous to do maths in the jungle?

2162. Why did the farmer plant sugar cubes?

2163. Why did the little girl eat bullets?

2164. Why is a robber strong?

2165. Why was the invisible mother upset with her invisible child?

2166. Why are Egyptian children good children?

2167. Why do werewolves do well at school?

2168. Why did the elephant wear sunglasses?

2169. Why do dentists like potatoes?

2170. Why are vampires unpopular?

2171. Why do the hippies study the stars?

2172. Why do flies walk on the ceiling?

2173. Why did the nature lover plant bird seed?

2174. Why did the farmer plant old car parts in his garden?

2175. Why do gardeners hate weeds?

2176. Why does a baby duck walk softly?

2177. Why is it so wet in Great Britain?

2178. Why shouldn't you cry if your cow falls off a mountain?

2179. Why don't bananas snore?

2180. Why is a cat like a penny?

2181. Why did the lady mouse want to move?

2182. Why do squirrels spend so much time in trees?

2183. Why don't flies fly through screen doors?

2184. Why is the longest human nose on record only 11 inches long?

2185. Why did the farmer think he was the strongest man in the world?

2186. Why is the letter N the most powerful letter?

2187. Why is a kid who plays all day in a marathon like a phonograph record?

2188. Why is being fat not very funny?

2189. Why is a hot dog the best dog?

2190. Why is the Dracula family so close?

2191. Why does a dog have fur?

2192. Why do people buy things with their credit cards?

2193. Why did the hippie put his money in the refrigerator?

2194. Why was the shoe unhappy?

2195. Why can't a bicycle stand up by itself?

2196. Why do they say George Washington was an orphan?

2197. Why do they say George Washington couldn't swim?

2198. Why was George Washington like a fish?

2199. Why couldn't Humpty Dumpty be put together again?
2200. Why do wallets make so much noise?
2201. Why did the invisible man look in the mirror?
2202. Why does a chicken lay an egg?
2203. Why don't scarecrows have any fun?
2204. Why are identical twins like a broken alarm clock?
2205. Why is the number nine like a peacock?
2206. Why do you say that whales talk a lot?
2207. Why do hummingbirds hum?
2208. Why shouldn't you keep a library book on the ground overnight?
2209. Why doesn't it cost much to feed a horse?
2210. Why do elephants have trunks?
2211. Why couldn't anyone play cards on the ark?
2212. Why are comedians like doctors?
2213. Why can't an elephant ride a bicycle?
2214. Your uncle's sister is not your aunt. Who is she?

Answers

2001. Camouflage.
2002. Because it is pressed for money.
2003. They both test the pupils.
2004. Because money doesn't grow on trees.
2005. Because they indicate the 'weigh'.
2006. One is obliged to give it up.
2007. It makes him a little better.
2008. From chasing parked cars.
2009. Because you will meet plenty of wax (whacks).
2010. He was waiting to catch the train.
2011. Because she didn't want to go.
2012. Because he had a chip on his shoulder.
2013. In order to check his balance.
2014. You might get a big kick out of it.
2015. Because he holds on to the last.
2016. So he can button it up.
2017. Because it is between two eyes.
2018. He had forgotten to take the cigarette out of his mouth.

2019. From time to time it blows its top.

2020. Because it's a falsehood.

2021. Because it's just a notion.

2022. He drove a hearse.

2023. Because he had written to say he'd grown another foot.

2024. She was one in a thousand.

2025. Because it didn't know how to conduct itself.

2026. Because he has MP at the end of his name.

2027. Because he feeds the great.

2028. Because he lost his patience.

2029. Because nothing satisfies him.

2030. She wanted a big wedding.

2031. Because it goes with a rattle.

2032. Because he's lying.

2033. She couldn't spell properly.

2034. Because twice ten is twenty, and twice eleven is twenty-two (twenty too).

2035. They were both in their cars at the time.

2036. So he could break out.

2037. It was a single-decker.

2038. The photographer was a late developer.

2039. To 'cape' them warm.

2040. Because peel follows peel.

2041. Because he has such winning ways.

2042. Because it is likely to be terribly bawled.

2043. To go with her mink coat.

2044. Because they are both up to something.

2045. Because they're wearing their hair longer.

2046. Because it went right out of your head.

2047. Because he's lost his locks.

2048. She wanted to catch up on her sleep.

2049. In case he got a hole in one.

2050. Teeth.

2051. He was caught lying down on the job.

2052. Because the population is denser in towns.

2053. Because it's a dear little thing.

2054. It had people-pox.

2055. Because it is useless without powder.

2056. Because we cannot get on without them.

2057. They both contain r-a-t-s.

2058. Ten to one.

2059. Because they have panes.

2060. Because they are both tumblers.

2061. Because without it friends would be fiends.

2062. To make a good impression on the pillow.

2063. Because he liked cold pop.

2064. Because it is catching.
2065. To cover his head.
2066. He was always first away when school was over.
2067. A skye terrier.
2068. True. You come down with a cold—never up.
2069. Because he has been to sea.
2070. Because he is always for getting.
2071. Because tales come out their heads.
2072. Because it strengthens the calves.
2073. It sounded too fishy
2074. Because they don't mind if you stick your tongue out at them.
2075. She found the job very absorbing.
2076. Because where there's a will, there's a way.
2077. One can see the drift.
2078. Because she must be brought to.
2079. Because it's full of ups and downs.
2080. Because it is planted in the spring.
2081. Because you take it when you're run down.
2082. Because the chimney had the flue.
2083. Because it is so-lo.
2084. Because they are upright and grand.
2085. Because he makes scandals.

2086. It had an automatic changer.
2087. Because he would never lie.
2088. Because day breaks and night falls.
2089. Because they are always spinning.
2090. It kept going off when he was asleep.
2091. He had been told you have to stamp them or they won't get taken by the post office.
2092. He was a watchdog and wanted to wind himself up.
2093. Because they come in packs.
2094. Because they are full of baas.
2095. That's when Julius Caesar.
2096. Because he knew the Highway Code backwards.
2097. Because it's always tired.
2098. Because there are so many shamrocks in Ireland.
2099. They both have to be plucked.
2100. She wanted to play by ear.
2101. Because he can't digest - yet.
2102. Because he was on a hush-hush mission.
2103. Because the customer was in a hurry and told the waiter to step on it.

2104. So no one will find him out.

2105. Because although the first is in pity, he's always the last in help.

2106. It might run down and strike one.

2107. Because she ran away from the ball.

2108. Because he draws so much water.

2109. Because it is on the level.

2110. Because they are always ready to take tips from people.

2111. Because it has to be ground before it can be used.

2112. Because he didn't know if he was coming or going.

2113. The postman.

2114. Because it is the centre of light.

2115. Because he swept her off her feet.

2116. Because times flies anyway.

2117. He wanted to make a big splash.

2118. She wanted to see a waterfall.

2119. Because that's all they are worth.

2120. He wouldn't be caught dead there.

2121. The baby can't carry the mother.

2122. He wanted to get the inside story.

2123. To keep their pants up.

2124. Because it is full of lead.

2125. Because we can't get them free.

2126. Because you keep it under your hat.

2127. If you did, everything might slip your mind.

2128. He could—if you had one!

2129. It saw the weather strip.

2130. Because the label said "Wash and Wear."

2131. Because the horse was too heavy to carry.

2132. It was guaranteed to wear like iron.

2133. Because it ate haywire.

2134. Because it had crabs in its bed.

2135. Two feet are always sticking out.

2136. Because she was so refined.

2137. Because they go around in bunches.

2138. Because she wants to keep her Stockholm (stock home).

2139. The barefoot boy wears no shoes and the Eskimo wears snowshoes.

2140. To keep the sea tide (tied).

2141. Because she didn't want to hear their foul (fowl) language.

2142. Because you fascinate (fasten 8).

2143. Because he was always saying, "I owe (heigh-ho) Silver!"

2144. Because it was a sycamore (sick of more).

2145. Because every time it wanted something, its mother would say, "Neigh."

2146. Because a bargain (barkin') dog does not bite.

2147. To get to the other side.

2148. Because they've been checked.

2149. She wanted to write shorthand.

2150. First they say they will treat you, and then they make you pay for it.

2151. Because it's not nice to poke fun at someone else's expanse.

2152. Because she was so moody.

2153. Because he is lean.

2154. Because it's catching.

2155. Because sometimes the ayes (eyes) have it and sometimes the no's (nose).

2156. To find out why he wasn't all there.

2157. He heard that fuses blew.

2158. Because he is then a hoarse horse.

2159. He wanted to see something swell.

2160. She was worried because he was in such good spirits.

2161. If you add 4 and 4, you get 8.

2162. Because he wanted to raise cane.

2163. She wanted her hair to grow in bangs.

2164. Because he holds people up.

2165. Because he was always appearing.

2166. Because they respect their mummies.

2167. Because they give snappy answers.

2168. With all the silly elephant riddles around, he didn't want to be recognised.

2169. Because they are so filling.

2170. Because they are a pain in the neck.

2171. Because they are so far out.

2172. If they walked on the floor, someone might step on them.

2173. He wanted to grow canaries.

2174. He wanted to raise a bumper crop.

2175. Give weeds an inch and they'll take a yard.

2176. Because it is a baby and it can't walk, hardly.

2177. Because of all the Kings and Queens that reigned (rained) there.

2178. There's no use in crying over spilt milk.

2179. They don't want to wake up the rest of the bunch.

2180. Because it has a head on one side and a tail on the other.

2181. She was tired of living in a hole in the wall.

2182. To get away from all the nuts on the ground.

2183. Because they don't want to strain themselves.

2184. Because if it were 12 inches long it would be a foot.

2185. Because he raised a 600-pound pig.

2186. Because it is in the middle of TNT.

2187. Because he is long-playing.

2188. Because you can't laugh it off.

2189. Because it doesn't bite the hand that feeds it but feeds the one that bites it.

2190. Because blood is thicker than water.

2191. If it didn't, it would be little bare (bear).

2192. They get a charge out of it.

2193. He liked cold cash.

2194. Because his father was a loafer and his mother a sneaker.

2195. Because it is two-tired (too tired).

2196. He was the foundling father of his country.

2197. He was the foundering father of his country.

2198. He was the flounder of his country.

2199. Because he wasn't everything he was cracked up to be.

2200. Because money talks.

2201. To see if he still wasn't there.

2202. If she dropped it, it would break.

2203. Because they are stuffed shirts.

2204. Because they are dead ringers.

2205. Because it is nothing without its tail.

2206. Because they are always spouting off.

2207. Because they can't read music.

2208. Because in the morning it will be overdue (dew).

2209. Because a horse eats best when it doesn't have a bit in its mouth.

2210. Because they don't have pockets to put things.

2211. Because Noah sat on the deck.

2212. Because they keep people in stitches.

2213. Because he doesn't have a thumb to ring the bell.

2214. Your mother.